A Norfolk Soldier
in the First Sikh War

A Norfolk Soldier in the First Sikh War
Experiences of a Private of
H.M. 9th Regiment of Foot in the
Battles for the Punjab, India 1845-6

J. W. Baldwin

Including
A History of the Sutlej Campaign
Dec. 1845 – March 1846
by Gough & Innes

A Norfolk Soldier in the First Sikh War:
Experiences of a private of H.M. 9th Regiment of Foot in the battles for the Punjab, India 1845-6

Originally published in 1851 under the
title *Four Months' Campaigns In India*

Including: *A History of the Sutlej Campaign*
Dec. 1845 – March 1846
by Gough & Innes

Published by Leonaur Ltd

FIRST EDITION

Material original to this edition
copyright © 2005 Leonaur Ltd

ISBN (10 digit): 1-84677-031-9 (hardcover)
ISBN (13 digit): 978-1-84677-031-9 (hardcover)

ISBN (10 digit): 1-84677-023-8 (softcover)
ISBN (13 digit): 978-1-84677-023-4 (softcover)

http://www.leonaur.com

Publisher's Notes

In the interests of authenticity, the spellings, grammar and place names used have been retained from the original editions.

The opinions of the authors represent a view of events in which he was a participant related from his own perspective, as such the text is relevant as an historical document.

The views expressed in this book are not necessarily those of the publisher.

Contents

A Norfolk Soldier in the First Sikh War   9

A History of the Sutlej Campaign   71

A Norfolk Soldier
in the First Sikh War

Preface

For the last five years I have been repeatedly requested by my friends, to publish this little narrative, not only for their information, but also that of the Parents and Friends of such Soldiers as served in the War with the Seikhs, during the memorable campaign of 1845—6, and of the army now serving in India.

I have hitherto declined doing so from an impression that a work with such little pretension as mine would scarcely lie noticed, much less read with interest, amidst the host of well-written and spirited descriptions of Military Life, constantly issuing from the Press; but the objection has been met with in this way—that the above works are generally very expensive and too voluminous, especially those relating to India, and not, therefore, within the reach of that class for whose amusement and instruction this narrative is more particularly published. It embraces a brief account of the Climate, the Customs and Manners of the Natives, including the Author's Personal Adventures.

I cannot help expressing my surprise that such little public attention has been drawn to the first Seikh war, so memorable in its results, and which laid, as it were, that powerful nation at our feet; a campaign so replete with personal intrepidity; as severe a contested struggle as any on record, and won after hard fighting by the indomitable bravery of the British Soldier.

If there is any merit in this little work, it must be upon the score of its veracity; on that ground alone do I venture to usher it into the world; perhaps my humble narrative, from the very simplicity of its details, may throw more light upon the actual experience of a Soldiers Life on Foreign Service, than most of those gorgeous and certainly very beautiful literary productions upon the subject which have been given to the Public by some of our most distinguished writers.

In bidding adieu to the courteous reader, for the first time as an author, I beg leave to say that I carry with me into my retirement from a Military Life, the proud consciousness of having done my duty and assisted in the overthrow of the once powerful Seikhs, most certainly the bravest and best equipped soldiers in India, and which settled for ever, I trust, the supremacy of British valour in that country.

J. W. Baldwin
North Walsham.

Narrative
Army of the Sutlej
Camp, Lahore, March, 1846.

Dear Cousin,
    I received your very kind and welcome letter dated November 12th, 1845, and was most happy to find that you, and all my family and friends, were in good health. This inestimable blessing I still enjoy, notwithstanding the privations and hardships I have lately undergone, which I trust, with the blessing of God, I shall be enabled truthfully to depict in the subjoining detail of the late campaign.

    I am sure you all have been in great anxiety about me for some time past, for doubtless you have seen in your newspapers startling accounts from this country with which you anticipated my being in some measure identified. From the tardiness I evinced in writing, you probably inferred that I was numbered with the dead, seeing, as you must have done, by the despatches from India, that so many men of my regiment, as well as others, were killed in our encounter with the Seikhs. But Heaven be praised I am spared, after having waded through fearful carnage and bloodshed, with, I may truly say, wonderful strength and courage. I could not write till now, to inform you of my welfare, with any satisfaction.

    Had I written immediately after surviving the first or second battle, I might probably have fallen in the next; besides, my time and thoughts were so occupied, that I had not the means or opportunity of writing; but now I avail myself of this occasion to make ample amends for being so long silent.

I perceive by a newspaper I have recently received from London, that there has been a very grand cricket match at Swaffham, between the Marylebone club and yours; I am sorry my old townspeople were so shamefully beaten by the former.

We have had a much finer match here between the Seikhs and the British, which, after a long and sharp contest, terminated in favour of the latter. We did not get licked! like you Swaffhamites. You will perceive I was an excellent fielder in the game, to let every ball pass me; nevertheless, you see, I immortalized myself by not being bowled down nor stumped out leg before wicket. I had always said in a light hearted manner, prior to entering the field of battle, that neither ball, bullet, sword, nor spear, were yet made to kill me; and now I fancy it must indeed be true, since I have been a target to some thousands and tens of thousands, and yet remain unhurt.

You have from my pen a narrative of my former campaign in this country, in which I trudged about 1100 English miles; but in all that distance, I did not experience five per cent of the vicissitudes and hardships of soldiering as I have done in the late expedition.

My present thankful state of mind may be better imagined than described, while extracting the following from my crowded memory, and communicating the same to you and all my friends, viz., a summary of the campaign in question, which I feel assured, you, and all concerned, will appreciate as coming from the hand of an unsophisticated soldier, who hopes to merit the name of a genuine patriot, and I trust will not be deemed a braggadocio in presenting on paper an unvarnished tale of his adventures during the last four months.

Our regiment marched in divisions of two companies from Kussowlie,* down to Kalcah, at the foot of the hills, one division on November 17th, 1845, the others on the following days in succession.

The ruggedness of the road leading down the mountains, (in spite of European skill and labour to render them passable,) is not easily described; the declivity is so great in some parts, that it is painfully difficult to walk; besides, this inconvenience is augmented by the sight of such fearful precipices, and deep abysses, as to excite constant terror. The path, in many places, is very steep and fearfully narrow, and on one side rises an eminence of many score yards; on the other, is an abyss of equal depth; so that if we had been somewhat " boozy " and staggered a step or two out of the track, we must have inevitably perished. I therefore called it " The Britannia Temperance Walk."

By referring to my former narrative, you will find if was at this very time (March) last year, that I ascended these lofty regions, with other recruits, going to join our regiment; we had about seven or eight miles of up-hill work; and I began to think we were climbing into another world; it was the most fatiguing day's journey we met with during a march of four months from Chinsurah, near Calcutta, the British Capital of India.

We remained at Kalcah more than a week, during which time, the death of one of our serjeants took place, whose funeral was attended with the usual military honours.

On the 26th we left and proceeded on the line of march towards Meerut, (a station) from whence Her Majesty's 29th regiment came to relieve us. Within a week after our departure from the hills, snow fell, which was rather a cold reception for that regiment, the men of which suffered very much at first from the inclemency of the weather, as they

---

*A Station on the Himalaya Mountains.

had been previously quartered in one of the hottest stations in India, (Meerut.) It was excessively cold before we left, but the snow had not reached us, though we could plainly see it on the " Snowy Range," at a great distance.

We feel the cold far more severe in this country than you do in England. The climate here is tropical, the heat is intense nine months in the year, and the blood becomes very thin, our bodies altogether very much relaxed, and every pore distended, consequently the cold is the more piercing during the other three months, and more especially at night. Though we feel the cold here very keenly, I do not pretend to say it is ever so severe as snowy and frosty weather in England, but if a breath of air blows from the heavens, one must be acutely sensible of it, on those prodigious high mountains, which I described to you last year. On the plains, snow has never yet been seen that I can hear of from those who have travelled thousands of miles about the country.

When I commenced writing I had no thought of occupying such a space in giving you an account of the weather and climate, I shall only therefore say briefly from my own experience, that every thing but cold is in extremes here; the heat intense, the rain floods, the winds hurricanes, and the hailstones sometimes, I dare not say how large, lest you should think I take the license of a traveller. But what I always behold with reverence and awe, and at the same time with pleasure, is the lightning; it is not that offensive glare of light which I have often seen in England and on board ship, but a beautiful fire which plays amongst the clouds and passes from one part of the heavens to another, in every direction, and in one continued vibration.

A few days marching brought as to Umballah, (a station) where we halted, and paraded one day in full reviewing order; shortly afterwards we joined the Umballah force, and had a jolly good sham fight for about five hours, under the command of Major General Gilbert; Sir Henry Hardinge, the Governor-general of India, Sir Hugh Gough, the Commander-in-chief of the forces in India, and a multitude of Staff Officers were present; also, a distinguished nobleman. Prince Waldemar, of Prussia, with his suite of officers and attendants, being on a tour through the British Empire in India, happened to arrive at our head quarters here and seemed to take great pleasure and interest in seeing our warlike display on this occasion.' I imagine this bit of fun (sham fight) was to get us juvenile soldiers inured to the smell of powder and smoke, technically "teaching the young idea how to shoot."

After our return, however, from this brigade field-day, the prevalent topic of discourse throughout our camp was, that something was brewing, or a storm arising somewhere, but where we could not conceive. Our predictions were verified, for only a few days subsequently, (December 10th) we received orders to be in readiness to march next morning towards the Punjaub, or the country of the Five Rivers, which created much excitement in this station, forming a depot in each respective regiment, where we left behind all the women and children, and the sick and debilitated men who were pronounced by the medical officers unfit for actual service.

We, as effective men having made the preliminary arrangements for campaigning, started next morning accordingly to go on expedition with the Umballah force, to repel an expected Invasion by the Seikhs, or rather to impede their further progress in our territory, should they then have crossed the river Sutlej, till we should have from other stations in Bengal an adequate force to combat them. Our small force consisted of Her Majesty's 3rd Light Dragoons, a few troops of Light Horse Artillery, the 31st, 80th, and our regiment of Infantry, together with some Native Cavalry and Infantry; in all, about 9000.

We hastened towards the Punjaub by forced marches of about 30 miles a-day, along roads of heavy sand, which indeed was hard work for the strongest of us; the marches being so long and fatiguing, and more over, falling short of provisions, in consequence of our camp-followers' inability to keep pace with us, whose cattle, poor things, were nearly harassed out of their lives, and some actually died on the road.

On the 17th, her Majesty's 50th regiment, and some Sepoys from Loodianah, (a station) joined us.

Next morning, (18th) we struck our tents about four o'clock, and moved off; the Artillery and Cavalry were sent on in front in skirmishing order, as the Governor-general and Commander-in-chief had, the previous day, received intelligence from our spies, that the enemy was coming to meet us, we heard the report of guns in front, several times, but no engagement took place.

We marched all, that day, nearly broiled beneath the scorching rays of the sun, and almost choked with clouds of dust, so dense that we could scarcely see each other in the ranks. A few of our men, having weak eyes, had now their sight so impaired by the dust and sand, that they were obliged to go into hospital for medical treatment. Probably you may have heard of the "Acting Corporal," sleeping with one eye open; now I can assure you I have found it a great convenience and comfort at times, marching with one eye open and the other closed, each eye alternately.

You cannot form any idea of what we endured on the march, having nothing to eat or drink until about three o'clock, p.m., when we halted close to a tank of water, where we all got a hearty drink, for which I was as thankful as if the beverage had been so much ale or porter, notwithstanding its being very indifferent water. This tank bore resemblance to a horse-pond in England; in it were elephants, camels, horses, and bullocks; dozens of our Bheestie-wallahs* walked in above their knees to procure the clearest of the water for us. When all the troops were supplied with a sufficient quantity, we resumed the march, and reached the camp (Moodkee) in about an hour's time when, to our discomfiture, there was only half a drachm of liquor for each man, being all that had arrived at the camp.

We piled arms, and took off our accoutrements, and were just in the act of pitching such tents as had arrived, when a mounted Aide-de-camp came galloping full speed to announce that the enemy was bearing down upon us rapidly.

We flew to arms instantly. There were several men who had taken off their jackets, and had not even time to put them on; and although in a state of exhaustion, we quickly formed parade, and seemed anew invigorated with the prospect of soon being in the midst of battle, which was our darling hope.

It was quite surprising to see with what nimbleness we now repaired to the scene of action, treading over ploughed ground, passing through corn fields, and leaping over numerous small bushes and clumps in our passage; sometimes we had to file in the front and rear, in order to pass the larger thickets.

The enemy were supposed to consist of about 15,000 Infantry, the same force of Cavalry, and 40 guns. They had taken up a position so as to screen themselves behind a thick jungle.

Our small force, about 14,000, including natives, was

* *Native Water-carriers.*

formed into divisions and brigades, Artillery, Cavalry, and three Infantry divisions.

Cannonading commenced on both sides, sometime ere we (Infantry) could get up. The 5th brigade, consisting of my own corps and two regiments of Sepoys★ forming part of the 3rd Infantry division, being on the extreme left of the army, were the last engaged. Whilst the other divisions were in action, we took up a position just where the enemy was expected to come. At this time the sable curtain of night had fallen, so that the enemy could not discover the exact strength of our force; and in order that they should not, our division, apart from the others, received orders to lie down, in so doing, we were sheltered from a most tremendous shower of bullets, which whistled over us.

The peculiar sounds of the variety of balls whizzing above our heads, the various distances from us, the faint sounds of our bugles and the enemy's tum-tums★★, produced very beautiful music, blended with the noise or thunder of the cannonade, and the musketry of both parties. Being neuter awhile, I could distinguish the different sounds. My position reminded me of a musician in a band, who, when he comes to a part in his music, "tacit," enjoys an opportunity of hearing the harmonious and melodious sounds of such instruments as are playing, but when engaged and his attention, drawn to his own part, he loses the rich melody which floats around him. You cannot form an adequate idea of the splendid music produced by instruments of war when well performed, and we had to play well, otherwise lose the game.

Notwithstanding the Seikhs being most gloriously peppered by the divisions on our right, they neared us who were impatiently waiting to be at them, anxious to mark

★ *Native Infantry in our Service*
★★ *Drums*

some with "Britannia." The enemy expected they had had all our force contending with them, and were now endeavouring to get in the rear of our army; had they succeeded, not a man of us could have escaped; being butchered on the field was inevitable.

But when they came near to our line, we up and at them to their surprise and dismay; thus we kept up an incessant fire for some minutes, the barrel of my firelock got so hot that I could hardly bear it in my hand, insomuch as I had to load with the muzzle placed on the cuff of my jacket. We had with us some veterans, who declared they never before heard such splendid file-firing, not even at Waterloo, nor in the Peninsular war. We directed our fire very low, so it did great execution, when, luckily for us, the enemy's bullets came teeming over our heads as thick as hailstones; if we had been mounted on stilts they would have knocked us off, I dare say, for now one of our men had a musket shot pass through the top of his cap, but it did not touch his head; at this time the balls seemed to rend the very atmosphere above us. It appears that our unexpected fire paralyzed the Seikhs, and finding great gaps in their ranks, they retreated in confusion, leaving behind them 17 pieces of brass cannon, I suppose for us to fight them with at some future time.

Now our bugles in every direction sounded the cease-firing, and as soon as the guns left off talking, we cheered, and our cavalry charged; who found that some of the enemy had crept into bushes, and others had climbed up trees, where our men could not get at them with their swords, but resorted to their carbines and shot some of the runagates.

The Lancers were wanted then, they could have picked the enemy out of the bushes, and fetched them down from the trees. I must tell you, it was our division that put the enemy to flight. But before I proceed any further, I will relate a very remarkable incident that occurred with one of the native regiments (26th) forming a part of our brigade.

On an expedition in 1841—2 this regiment and ours amalgamated on one fighting occasion, one file of our men, and a file of theirs, placed in the ranks alternately; the two regiments thus combined fought at the forcing of the celebrated Khyber pass, acting in perfect sympathy with each other, and became greatly attached; the natives ever esteeming it an honour to fight collaterally with the men of our regiment, in whose invincibility they placed so much reliance, and from the familiarity existing between them, they technically called their regiment "The Little Ninth," since that expedition. However, they have been stationed at Loodianah, with Her Majesty's 50th corps, and when appointed to that regiment's brigade, broke out into mutiny, protesting they would not fight in any brigade but ours; their request was acceded to, and great credit is due to them above many other Sepoys for their consummate bravery, not only at Moodkee, but at Ferozeshuhur and Sobraon.

In returning to the defeat of the enemy at Moodkee, where our division opened its fire on them, we subsequently found they had fallen in dozens, so that when our cavalry charged them, some of their horses fell over ridges of dead bodies.

After the cavalry returned from the charge, and perfect tranquillity prevailed all around, the Governor-general, Commander-in-Chief, and Staff Officers, congratulated our army on having vanquished and overcome the proud Seikhs for the first time, as they never before had been beaten. They came up to our regiment, and technically speaking, daubed us over with "soft soap," highly applauding us for our valour in dispersing the enemy in the manner we did. Then our whole force, taking the time from the Commander-in-Chief, gave three thundering cheers, in consequence of having achieved a most glorious victory at Moodkee. The illustrious hero, Prince Waldemar, with his attendants, took part in the action, and distinguished himself in a most brilliant manner.

We now piled arms, and remained in bivouac until about one o'clock, a.m., (19th) during which time our wounded were sought after and conveyed to camp; among them was one of my boots.

It is a most singular fact, that while file-firing, I felt a smart jerk of my foot and leg, forcing the former against my neighbour's; at first I wondered what was the matter, but feeling no pain, I still kept on firing. When I got to camp I found the Seikhs had tried to leave me barefoot, for there was a small piece of the sole of my stout "ammunition" boot cut away by a musket ball, resembling the cut of a half-moon chisel; rather a close shave, an inch higher would have made me grin, not laugh, as I was forced to do at the discovery, Although my boot was thus wounded, I did not discharge it with a pension till worn out by length of service.

Several of our men were wounded in their feet and legs in this engagement. An Irishman on my left was hit by a half-spent musket ball, cutting through his trousers and shirt, but it did not penetrate his body, owing to an empty stomach, yet it was a pretty hard knock for him I have no doubt, and we ought not to smile at another's misfortune, but really we could not refrain when he writhed and twisted himself about exclaiming, "Mr. O'Connor, (an Officer of our company,) I'm kilt! I'm kilt!" "Then lie down my man," coolly rejoined the officer.

It is with great reluctance I here notice two men of our regiment—a thousand curses on the serjeant who enlisted them—one was what we call a Liverpool Irishman, the other, a West Country-man, neither of them very bright you will find, for whatever trouble and pains were taken to instruct them in their drill, they could not learn it. I remember when practising at the target one time at Kussowlie, neither of these fellows hit it once, which so enraged the drill serjeant, that he placed them only twenty yards off; they then did not touch it. Whether from pusillanimity or utter stupidity, I can't say, but in this first engagement they would not even try to shoot at the enemy, and as soon as we commenced the action, fell to the rear and went back to the camp, where, of course, the guard took them into custody as prisoners.

Next day they were paraded in front of the regiment, but being young men, the commanding officer merely gave them a good lecture, which I dare say was the same as French to them, making little or no impression on their weak minds; he might just as well have whistled jigs to milestones. After questioning them a good deal, if I remember aright, one said in vindication of his conduct, "he did'nt like shooting folks!" the other said "why for I shoot they Seikhs an kill un, they did'nt kill I." The best man living could not command his temper with these two, what to term them I don't know, except automatons, so we were not surprised at our Colonel using rather scurrilous language, calling them the greatest fools, and positively swearing he would punish them with severity at the end of the campaign, but he did not live to carry out his threat, for two days after, he was killed at Ferozeshuhur. Had he, however, survived all the battles, he would have seen that they did not receive a medal nor batta-money, which we expect to have to the amount of £8. I will now revert to circumstances more soldier-like, however painful to relate.

In the action we had killed and wounded, of all ranks, about 900, among whom was Major-General Sir John McCaskill, K.C.B., K.H., of our regiment, killed by a ball passing through his chest, whom we interred next day.

General Sale also finished his career at Moodkee, he who so laudably distinguished himself in the Afghanistan war in the years 1841—2, an account of which I remember reading in the newspaper when I lived at Mr. D. Sewell's, of North Walsham. I sat up the best part of the night reading the details of that bloodshed, and I remember, as if it were only yesterday, asking my shopmate, (John A,) if he would like to have been there to participate in that apparent rough sport, he replied in the negative;" I should," I rejoined, "for in our confined sphere, we know literally nothing of the world, and are dying of ennui." Though I was totally ignorant of the horrors of warfare, yet my reflections on what I had just been reading, excited in me a feeling of deep sympathy and sorrow for my poor fellow creatures who had sacrificed their lives fighting, not only for themselves, but for you and I; the same sympathy I felt for the survivors, who most probably would soon again have to meet the contending foe amidst the awful work of death; at the same time little did I think I should ever be in a similar situation.

"When lying in bivouac on the field heaven knows what those poor fellows suffered who had not their jackets on, when we, being clad, were almost perished with. cold. The night here is as cold as the day is hot. Here too, we felt the sharp pinch of hunger; now if you can't altogether fancy the state of my mind at the time, you may the painful condition of my body, when you consider I had been marching all day a distance of about 40 miles, without so much as seeing, (setting aside eating,) a particle of food, and then what a luxury to be driven into the field of battle, and, if I may use the words, get a belly-full of hard fighting.

The Commander-in-Chief being satisfied that the enemy had had sport enough for once, gave orders for us to quit the field, which we quickly did, and reached our camp about two o'clock a.m. How glad we were on finding our tents pitched ready to protect us from the oppressive dews that had fallen during the night, and to our exceeding great joy the commissariat had arrived, so we had a profusion of grog, the effect of which, blended with the exciting thoughts of the past, stimulated us to such a degree, that we fancied, though but a handful of men, we could drub the whole force of the black d—ls of Seikhs. We also found (what immeasurably added to our comfort) that a native Chief, on amicable terms with us, had supplied our camp with provisions, and our bubbagees* had prepared some food for us "a dish of pillao," an a-la-mode Indian dish, made with meat, rice, and spices boiled together, which I assure you was very acceptable at the time. This comfortable repast in some degree renovated our bodies, and restored us to our usual strength and vigour, for we were in fact fast losing our stamina through privation, not having had any good food .for the last four days. At that time it might well be said of us "a full breast and an empty stomach," according to the popular phraseology of soldiers,

> "Our hearts were fill'd with great delight!
> Our stomachs were in dreadful plight!"

But to keep us from absolutely starving, we regaled on elephant's victuals, and execrable stuff it was sure enough; we had to pick out the straw and filth, before it was at all fit for mastication. We were then, however, like ostriches, could digest almost anything. I imagine I shall never be very fastidious, as regards my diet, when calling to mind "the quadrupeds' cakes." Knowing that other food was not to be had, I swallowed it contentedly, though not with much enjoyment, as you may easily imagine. After, in this instance, partaking of a good supper of wholesome food,

---

* *Native cooks.*

(the pillao) we, that were off duty, reposed for a short time in harness, with our fire-locks loaded and bayonets fixed by our sides in readiness to turn out with alacrity, should the enemy be disposed to molest us. At day break we arose and sallied out in fighting order, taking up a position some distance from the camp; but the enemy did not appear, they had already learned a trick worth two of that; they would not again quit their entrenchments to meet us, having been once bitten by so doing. At mid-day we returned to camp, and late in the evening were reinforced by two regiments from the hills. Her Majesty's 29th and the East India Company's 1st European Infantry, with a few heavy guns.

Next day (20) I went on out-lying picket, and the ensuing morning, about four o'clock, came off duty; this being Sunday; and how great the difference; while you are going quietly to church, we go rushing remorselessly to slaughter our fellow men, or to be slain ourselves. I have not been into a church myself for a very long time, but have often heard prayers read, although only once during the last four months, and then we most needed them, being every now and then in battle, and some poor souls hurried into eternity. From the time the first shot was fired up to the present period, my constant prayer has been, "From our enemies defend us O Lord ! Our whole trust is in thee." I am happy to say that I always remembered the Sunday from other days, but I have been sometimes amused at many of our fellows disputing about the day of the week and month, upon which any remarkable event occurred, and deciding the matter by counting their fingers.

Our army sallied forth leaving the tents standing, and a small guard over the baggage, and all the wounded (excepting my boot and another's cap) were left in a small fort near our position.

We proceeded towards the Seikhs' camp at Ferozeshuhur,

and reconnoitering parties were sent in front of the main force; at daylight we had reached the spot where we fought on the 18th, affording us an opportunity of seeing the result of that ever memorable night; what an awful scene to witness, so many once proud Seikhs -hurried into eternity.

On examining some of them it struck me, that being wounded and unable to walk, they threw aside their arms and accoutrements, took off their jackets, turned them inside out, and thus putting them on again, crept into the bushes, where they died from the severity of the cold and loss of blood. Only think of the shrewdness of these people on the very verge of death. You must know their jackets were of bright scarlet cloth, trimmed with white lacing and lined with blue. Hence, no doubt, their motive for turning them, was to avoid being noticed in case we passed over the ground while they still existed, whereas, if not turned, they would have been very conspicuous, and likely to be observed by us through the thickets. I remarked to my comrades at the time, that they died complete *"turncoats!"*

There were several of our men lying dead on the field, it being dark at the time of battle, many had straggled away from their respective corps after receiving a wound, and not found when the other wounded were taken to camp. We made it our duty to bury all the Europeans, digging graves for them with our bayonets, and scrapping away the mould with our hands; the soil not being very firm, we found the task easier than might have been expected.

After all were interred, we resumed the march, and about two o'clock p.m. General Littler with his small force, about 5000, including natives from Ferozepore (a station) joined us, which consisted of Her Majesty's 62nd regiment, several regiments, of Native Cavalry and Infantry, with a corresponding proportion of Artillery. Our now formidable force (about 20,000, including natives) was formed into divisions and brigades; about two hours afterwards we attacked the Seikhs' entrenched camp.

Our brigade formed the reserve of the left division, and met with some monstrous sharp work, as you will perceive. Cannonading commenced with both parties, nearly an hour before the Infantry had a chance of using their shooting sticks. The 62nd regiment's brigade formed the advance of the left division, and were the first to charge an immense battery of guns, and of heavy battering calibre, which had opened a fierce fire upon us. Meantime our brigade advanced to within range of the enemy's long shots, which came rolling down upon us, though with halfspent velocity, and being very large we could perceive them as they bounded along, in time to open out, and let them pass through our ranks.

We were greatly annoyed here by the bushes, as we were at Moodkee. I think verily these Seikhs must bear some affinity to the "bush rangers" in New Zealand, from their choosing these blackguard places to fight in.

As we neared the camp their shots became dangerous, making a few gaps in our line, and, when arriving at where the balls came with greater force, we were ordered to lie down, which we did flat as pancakes! as you may readily guess. In this position we remained a short time, the balls bounding over by hundreds, but not injuring us in the least. But soon, however, our bugles sounded the "arise," then we rose and advanced a little nearer to the scene of action, when the balls came whish! whish! whish! over us in all directions, and I regret to say severed the heads, legs, and wings of some of our poor unfortunate fellows.

Again we were ordered to lie down, to which you may suppose we felt no objection. Our position at the time reminded me of being caught in a very heavy tempest some distance from home, and finding a place of shelter on the spot, keeping there till the storm abated, and afterwards proceeding home dry and comfortable. And so we were in hopes the enemy would diminish their fire upon us ere long, that we might advance nearer without incurring such risk as the present circumstances foreboded. But if we had been sheltered there till this time, to all appearances their fire would have been as furious as ever. While in that position we laid listening to the apparent desperate work with the advance brigade, then assailing the tremendous battery in front of us an incessant fire was kept up for sometime by our people, but hearing a cessation we surmised that the 62nd were sick of shooting and had had recourse to their bayonets; shortly afterwards, seeing them return so orderly and deliberately as they did, we thought they had carried the battery, and that others were then directed toward us.

I began to fear that I should not have any sport whatever, but had come on a "wild-goose chase." But I afterwards found the aspect of things much darker than I had conjectured, for the men of the 62nd were cut down by dozens at the bores of the cannon; the survivors, poor fellows, after cutting and pelting away for some minutes witnessing numbers of their comrades falling around, were obliged to retire burning with revenge; as they passed by our right flank, they gave us to understand there were "breakers ahead" which indeed was true enough, for when our squadron sailed up to them, it was in a measure wrecked.

Our General having been killed at Moodkee, Brigadier Wallace was appointed to command our brigade, who was killed shortly after giving us the word "charge;" and as we were doubling towards the volcanic battery which made such fearful devastation amongst the 62nd regiment, our Colonel's horse was shot from under him, but he, nothing daunted, led us on foot, sword in hand. He (Colonel Taylor) was well known to be as brave officer, and, I regret to say, fell a victim in this memorable charge.

Two days after we found his lifeless body lying on the field, clasped in the arms of a soldier of my company; from the position in which the two dead bodies laid, we conjectured that, the former was wounded, in the first instance, and the latter was in the act of carrying him to the rear, when a shower of grape shot killed them both.

There were also nearly twenty others of our regiment lying round, them; several of whom had been cut and mutilated in a most frightful manner by the treacherous foe during the night. Coming to the, point, is a favourite maxim, and I can now say, that for once in my life I have been obliged, to come to the point, and that too of the sword and bayonet.

Our loss in the charge was considerable, especially in the left wing of the regiment, consisting of my company, three others and part of another; the greater part of the right wing happily escaped the tremendous fire from this terrific battery, and the mournful result of storming, being detached from us, and engaged in setting fire to the, enemy's camp, and exploding some of their magazines; scores of poor fellows, were cut down by discharges from this prodigious battery, in the same manner as the richest flower (wheat) in England falls from the scythe.

The Seikh Artillery, with whom we contended, were picked men, both for valour and size ; they were indeed gigantic, their usual stature being from six feet to six feet three inches, muscular and active in proportion. We were only like Lilliputians in comparison with those huge monsters, and I marvel they did not kill us all and swallow us slick out of the way. Had they been without tasting food for awhile, I am sure we should have been but a scanty meal for their numerous army, but fortunately they had been well fed, or possibly we might have become their prey. Yet I do not wish you to think them cannibals; on the contrary, respecting their diet, they are inclined to fastidiousness, never eating beef or pork, nor does any Indian eat pork excepting ham, which is exported from England, and he evades the law by calling it "European mutton." Playing thus given you a slight description of the Seikhs' position, you will observe it was not eating but fighting with us.

We lost lots of men before we got to the enemy's principal battery, for we were pushed, as it were, into the lion's mouth; when we did reach it the gunners resorted to their tol-wols* and we our bayonets, then came the "tug of war"—with clashing of steel in earnest.

In describing, to the best of my ability, the most desperate conflict which then took place, I might present to your imagination such scenes of horror as were never before witnessed in this country, although the Indians are for ever at war, either with the British or among themselves.

What a picture of horror I beheld when we and the Seikhs were straining every nerve to deeds of barbarity, wholly bent on mutual destruction, wielding sanguinary weapons, swords, and bayonets.

The ground in a few minutes was sprinkled with the blood of hundreds of brave men. With what anguish of heart I heard the moanings of the wounded and the shrieks of the dying, yet, at such time, compassion is swallowed up in the wild uproar of fierce passion and deadly animosity.

* *Very large swords*

Those overgrown brutes of artillery men had great advantage over us, and they fought with unusual courage, many of their lives being bought at the price of ours, i.e, when some of our men plunged their bayonets into the Seikhs, they held them fast by the sockets with their left hands, and cut our men's heads off with their massive tol-wols; with deep regret I saw several of my comrades thus killed, and in my first exploit with the bayonet I was within a day's march of sharing the same fate, but, providentially, I had the presence of mind to relinquish the left hand grasp of my musket as soon as the bayonet had penetrated the body of my antagonist, who, as I expected, made a dexterous cut at me, but with no effect. I extricated my bayonet instantly, when he fell, muttering something which I could not understand, and soon expired. I did not stay to close his eyes, but kept the game alive with my then tried taw, not a marble one, but a steel one.

Till now I was unconscious of having spilt the blood of any of the enemy, though I fired at them times enough, both at Moodkee, and on the present occasion, ere we came to close quarters, to annihilate; a whole' battalion, provided my exertions had been successful. I shall for ever entertain a most lively recollection of that not "cricket match" but "skivering match."

Here I absolutely saw the dead, as it were, killing the living. This may seem incredible to you, but. to be more explicit: when a man of ours succeeded in burying his bayonet in the Seikh's body he considered him hors-de-combat, but the enemy, (in his dying agonies, and determined to sell his life as dearly as possible,) grasping the bayonet with the left hand and mustering a last effort, generally succeeded in dealing such a blow with, his tol-wol from the right-hand, as to lay his assailant prostrate, and thus both fell mortally wounded in the fearful struggle. Just at the time we had butchered all the gunners of the battery, cries of "Cavalry coming" rang in our ears; we were then in a very awkward situation, higgledy-piggledy, helter-skelter among the guns; after having therefore spiked a few of them, we withdrew to a more open spot, where we might better defend ourselves against any sudden attack.

Here we were destitute of a commander, till the only surviving captain of our regiment, who, by the bye, was severely wounded in the arm, (a son of the Rev. Borton, of Blofield, Norfolk,) took the command, and ordered us to form square and resist, cavalry, at the same time exclaiming, "your colours, men! for God's sake, men, guard your colours!" which, I believe, we were resolved to. do to a man, without such marked injunction from our new commander.

At this time night came on, and the enemy's Cavalry had not the courage to come up for fear of being taken by surprise in the dark. We remained for some time in square, but finding the Cavalry were not forthcoming we, retired, formed companies, and numbered off by files, sections, and sub-divisions; our whole line numbered 110 files, which made 220 men, out of about 800, prior to the charge; the others, not being present, we thought were either killed or wounded, knowing that full 250 must have fallen at the battery with us.

Shortly afterwards an aide-de-camp came, who inquired what regiment we were? Being told the remains of the 9th, he informed us that he had just left 300 or thereabouts of our men in a part of the enemy's camp which cheered us not a little. In this position, we continued till further orders, beholding the Seikhs' camp in a blaze, which presented a most striking and sublime spectacle; torrents of fire illuminated the horizon to a great distance, the stars in the heavens seemed eclipsed, and repeated explosions of powder mines, rendered the scene awful beyond description.

The Seikhs' entrenched camp was about a mile in length, and half a mile in breadth, including within its area the village of Ferozeshuhur, with upwards of 100 guns, half of them of heavy battering calibre, dispersed over their position, which was entrenched and defended by European skill. The enemy's cannonade made great ravages throughout our force; our Artillery being unable to silence theirs, and our Cavalry force very weak, although the 3rd Dragoons did wonders., but the great weight of the battle fell upon us, (Infantry) and we had succeeded in carrying a part of the Seikhs' entrenchments before retiring to wile away the night.

The aide-de-camp who so recently left us went back to our other men, telling them of our safety; three of whom (grenadiers) soon found their way to us, stating that the right wing had been, and were then, setting fire to the Seikhs' camp, exploding magazines, and had sustained scarcely any loss. These men were as pleased to see us as we were them, for they had great fear of our being killed, and the colours of the regiment lost, which were with us.

We laid upon our oars as it were during night, but the serpents of Seikhs still stinging us a little; there was one in particular of their big guns making great havoc among us. As we laid, every few minutes we heard the. crush of some poor fellow. The gallant old 80th regiment and the 1st European Light Infantry, were next to us, and hearing them bustling about, we jumped up and seized our arms, but were ordered to lie down again; they were only going to silence the above-mentioned gun, which they succeeded in capturing and then retired.

About one or two o'clock, a.m., the enemy ceased firing upon us altogether, and began to shift their position with the design of baulking us of our intended attack at daylight.

I need hardly say I spent a most miserable night, in the early part of which my ears were greeted every few moments with the roaring noise of large cannon; the deep hollow booming sound excited within me a very melancholy sensation, and being at no great distance from the river Sutlej, the water conveyed the report as far as the hills, a great distance off, which echoed and re-echoed in one prolonged and dismal reverberation; added to this, we were saluted every quarter or half hour with hideous and unearthly yells from the enemy's camp, with the beating of their tum-tums, followed in the interval by heavy cannonading for a few minutes.

During this time the Governor-General and other officers visited us, for the purpose of cheering our spirits, saying we must and were sure to drub the Seikhs, when daylight appeared.

As paddy says, the morning part of the night not a sound was heard, save that of the sentries, whose duty it was to keep us from slumber; our arms were piled, and we lying on the cold damp ground, having nothing to wrap round ourselves to keep us warm. In order to imbibe warmth we huddled close together somewhat similar to the schoolboys' game, "mend-the-muck-heap," and just as we might be getting tolerably warm and dosing off, the sentries would, according to their duty, arouse us, and in an instant we were on our feet, seized our. arms, and arranged ourselves in fighting order, not knowing but the enemy was really coming- upon us.

This occurred frequently during the night; don't you think it was cold comfort? I had often said, when being but little troubled, "there is no rest for the: wicked," and if that be true,' there, were none good in our whole army, for we all were in the same sad and uncomfortable predicament. I think the Seikhs, too, might be classed with us, for I am sure they had even less rest than ourselves.

Just at daybreak our commisariat supplied us with a small portion of grog, which cheered our blades a bit. You see we kept our spirits up by pouring spirits down, when opportunity offered. Having braced up our nerves with brandy, we formed in battle array; our big dogs then commenced barking, and when the enemy got theirs not only to bark but bite, we shouted and made a glorious charge, and succeeded in expelling the Seikhs from' their camp, excepting a few of their Artillery-men, most determined fellows, who stood by their gun firing grape at us till the very last, but did not give themselves time to ram well the cartridges, so their courageous effort was not very successful; and when our line had nearly closed on them, they absolutely sprang forward sword in hand to meet us, and of course were soon shot.

Here again I was conscious of shedding blood, but I hope I shall not.be reproached for such barbarity, as it was solely in self-defence, and you know "self-preservation is the first law of nature."

I am proud to say, that the gallant old 9th, (my own corps) the pride and glory of East Norfolk, was the firsthand foremost in this brilliant charge, led by the Governor-General and his son, quite a youth.

I afterwards heard some men of the 29th regiment remark that they thought us mad drunk when we led the van in this charge, and said they had to run like the d—l to overtake' our brigade. Shortly after the enemy's discomfiture the same: party as before mentioned, "soft soaped" us again to the old tune. After weakening our lungs in loud cheers, triumphing over our achievement, we were permitted to plunder the enemy's camp. I went in search of water, and found some, (very sweet) which conduced more to my comfort at the time than all the wealth in their camp, not withstanding its being immensely rich with chests full of gold and silver, and bale after bale of silks, cashmere shawls, and other valuable merchandise.

Many soldiers that were not engaged at the aforesaid battery the previous night, got into the Seikhs' camp at that time, and loaded horses and bullocks with the specie, but I know only one man, and he of our regiment, who succeeded in keeping his prize. He has since told me that he took a splendid horse (an Arab) from a Seikh officer, whom he killed, loaded it with plunder, and, favoured by the darkness of the night, made good his way to Ferozepore, and there left his booty with a soldier's wife of the 62nd regiment, but returned to his duty in good time without exciting any suspicion. He also: told me his intention was to transmit the money by Installments to his friends in Ireland, and afterwards intended returning to the ould country and marrying the flower of Killarney, spend the remainder of his days in peace and in the enjoyments of matrimony, with all its concomitant blessings, amidst the honours of a retired veteran.

The other soldiers who took such pains in loading cattle with the shining stuff, steered with their booty to our camp at Moodkee, and there it was seized by the Prize Agents, and the captors sent to the right-a-bout, quick march, back to the battle field. In my further search about the camp, I found some oranges, which I enjoyed very much, whilst many of my comrades who went about carelessly to plunder, met with an untimely end, as there were at that time a number of the enemy secreted in the tents, most of whom we ultimately killed.

While I was exploring the camp, I met with a soldier of another corps, and we walked together, talking of our adventures, till we came to a handsome tent, inhabited by two females. My new friend, being an Irishman, exclaimed," the Lurrid his mercy upon us since the vimmin take up arms to murdther us." The elder woman was dead, and the younger was severely wounded, whom I could not behold without compassion; she was as beautiful a piece of mahogany as I had seen for a long time. She told us that she was the "fancy fair one of a Seikh chief, but we could scarcely understand what she said, neither did she us. We found her lying on a kind of couch in a magnificent tent lined throughout with silk, and the poles of which were of solid silver. These tents are impervious to the heat, the cold, the rain, and the dews. My friend paddy says to me, shall we shorten the pretthur crathur's life of misery," no don't kill her poor thing, I replied; "I suppose yer wud rather be afther kissin her thin killin her," rejoined he; he was right most unquestionably. The poor dying girl asked me for a little water, and very glad I was in having some in my tom-tom* to give her, and likewise an orange which I had in my haversack. Having drank, she gazed on me with an air of gratitude, as, on first seeing us enter, she expected no mercy; but you know I could not kill a woman even if my most inveterate foe.

I never desire to see another in the battlefield. I firmly believe a regiment of Amazons would have conquered the whole host of us. While we were in the tent, bugles in every direction sounded the "assembly," a sound well known to a soldier. My companion cried out " blood-a-nouns hark'ee be jabers, an tis fightin we'll be at agin, the black divils are not bate yet I'll ingage."

All the men ran railway pace, and fell in the ranks of their respective corps. It was not till at this time that all our regiment met together since the charge the preceding evening. This unexpected summons, as may be supposed, created powerful excitement throughout the army. We afterwards learnt that the enemy, in their retreat, met a re-inforcement of 30,000 men, accompanied by a vast

• *A tin for the use of soldiers on the line-of-march in this country*

number of "bull dogs," (heavy ordnance,) and a supply of ammunition, which encouraged them to turn right-a-bout and assail us again, with the view of annihilating us, and recapturing their camp.

Having approached our position within range of shot, their Artillery saluted us, and ours politely returned the compliment. An incessant fire was kept up between them for some time, whilst we, (all the Infantry) were lying in squares about the camp, until the enemy's fire became so destructive as to oblige us to shift our quarters. Thus we kept moving about for at least two hours.

As we were once marching in column from one part of the camp to another, in order to shun some of the worst of the enemy's, fire, we lost several men; one in particular was walking immediately behind me, when a cannon ball knocked off his head, dashing the blood, brains, and small particles of flesh amongst us.

Shortly after, at nearly spent long-shot struck Ensign Foster (who was carrying one of the colours) in the leg, knocking him down, I heard something, and looking behind me, I saw him jump up with the flag still in his hand, and soon he limped up to his place in the ranks,, uttering a curse on' the d—d brutes' of Seikhs for thus kicking his leg. What very strange looking beings some of us were just after the battle, having our faces and hands covered; with blood, mingled with dust and filth from all kinds of smoke; our clothes from head to foot painted all over; and our once white, now sable; belts besmeared with it. I should like then to have had my portrait taken by an artist, that I might show you the great difference between a fighting man in this country, and the clean, pipeclayed soldier in England, who is the object of some people's admiration.

Here Lieutenant Creagh, of my company, was; so knocked up through privation and fatigue, that he could not walk another step; what to do with him we could not conceive; if left behind he would most assuredly be killed. At length. strong and powerful old veteran of my company took him under one arm and thus carried him through the march. At one time we were driven quite out of the camp, but soon we succeeded in regaining possession; the enemy, notwithstanding, gained upon us rapidly, and I assure you we were filled with consternation and dismay at the fearful spectacle of death around us; not only one life, nor a hundred, nor a thousand, but myriads were lying about in all directions in the vicinity of the extensive camp in various forms of mutilation. Such a terrific spectacle, and the improbability of our escaping similar destruction, inspired us with an avenging spirit, insomuch that we would have rushed at the enemy with redoubled fury, had our commanders permitted it.

I now wanted the water that I gave away, not having a drop in my tom-tom, neither had any of my comrades, who, as well as myself, were famishing for the want of it; our mouths and lips became painfully blistered and parched from biting the cartridges, while clouds of dust, volumes of smoke, and the horrible stench emanating from the putrid bodies of the numerous slain, including camels, horses and bullocks, greatly added to our sufferings. I witnessed truly disgusting scenes arising from want of water, or something to drink, which I must decline mentioning here, but I will tell you all about it should I be spared to return to old England.

Eventually we came close to a well of water, around which we saw some Sepoys performing ablution with what we so dearly wanted to drink. Several of our corps, including myself, got leave, to quit the ranks to get some to quench our thirst with. Having arrived at the well, we had nothing wherewith to draw the water; the Sepoys had, but would not assist us, neither would they give us any drink of which they had a profusion, such as it was; we repeatedly asked them, but in vain, which you may suppose excited our indignation not a little; we consulted each other, and knowing the character of these people, a man of ours struck one of the fellows, knocking him into the well, while on the brink drawing up his jumbo★ of water, and threatened the other Sepoys in their language, that we would certainly serve them the same if they did not that instant give us where with to slake our thirst. We frightened them so much that they quickly handed us some, or rather it was a compound of blood and water; there might probably have been 20 or 30 wounded men in the well, who fell in during the preceding night. The water was tinged with blood, and of a very offensive smell. I put some powder in mine to purify it, before drinking, which made a most peculiar beverage. This gunpowder tea! I believe, strengthened me very much, but I had rather preferred a cup of good congou!

It did not signify where we went, the enemy's cannon balls were sure to find us out. While getting water; several men surrounding the well were shot. Having drank a sufficiency, and replenished our tom-toms we returned to the regiment. You will perhaps think us very cruel to kill that Sepoy, but I beg leave to say, that under such circumstances we thought no more of killing him than we should a Seikh, as we were persuaded he was, like most of the Sepoys, an enemy in disguise.

Only a part of those soldiers would fight for us at all, although they were in the field for that purpose. Hence several of their European Officers abandoned them, and joined our regiment and other European corps, stating

★*A small vessel made of either brass or copper, to contain two pints, which always accompany the Sepoy.*

that they could not get the "black rascals" to fight. To gratify my mind at that time, I should like to have stuffed all of them with gunpowder and blown them to the d—l.

After several hours sharp cannonading, our Artillery's ammunition was all expended, and they were obliged to fire blank cartridges in order to show fight; but it appears the enemy did not detect it. I then thought we were going to leeward indeed.

Sir Hugh Gough finding we were unable to beat the enemy back, ingeniously devised a plan formidable enough to frighten them; his stratagem was, placing all our Cavalry force behind the bushes, some distance off the camp. Being thus arranged, they extended about two miles. I must tell you the, bushes in this locality are almost as intricate as a maze. The battle at this crisis was decidedly in favour of the Seikhs, and as our last resource, the bugles sounded the "charge," when instantly all our Cavalry rushed out from their position, and being thus extended, there appeared to be thousands of them; and from the dense cloud of dust they occasioned, the enemy could not discover their weakness. Our having expected daily the arrival of the 9th and 16th Lancers, and seeing apparently such a strong force of horsemen, and unconscious at the time of the shrewd scheme of Sir Hugh's, the general cry throughout our Infantry was, that the 9th and 16th were come at last. "Look at them boys! there they go as fresh as daisies." We were all transported with ecstasy at the idea of their coming so timely. The officers brandished their swords, and we soldiers waved our bayonets and shouted from the top of our voices, "On, on to the charge ye brave! ye brave!" &c.

We Infantry prepared to resist the enemy's Cavalry, in case ours should be repulsed, but happily they were not; on the contrary, they routed the enemy, and took possession of all their guns and ammunition, making 91 captured in this battle.

We were surprised, and really amused, when the Cavalry returned from the charge, at finding they were only the 3rd Dragoons and native Cavalry, whose loss, you may guess, was considerable.

I must observe that our surviving army owe their safety to Sir Hugh Gough's superior Generalship, and the gallant conduct of the 3rd Dragoons. The gallant and noble General's conduct, and also that of the 3rd Dragoons, speaks for itself; any praise of mine would fall very far short of their merit. It is expected that every man does his duty in battle — I hope and believe every European fulfilled the duties of a soldier at Ferozeshuhur; yet, unfortunately, the gallant fellows who so bravely face death in their country's cause, enjoy little or no after-fame for their brilliant achievements, or receive any great emolument; while, through their (the men) consummate bravery, the officers receive encomiums, honours, and riches. However, as regards myself, I am truly thankful to have thus escaped the destructive hand of war. I scorn to boast, but you know I might have carved out a better fortune for myself, had I been deaf to the voice of honour, and swerved from the paths in which she bid me walk. Ambition led me from my dearest friends, my happy home, and my beautiful country; but I trust, by the aid of Providence, to return a wiser and a better man, with a patriot's true love to my Queen and fatherland.

About an hour after the defeat of the enemy we kept under arms, meanwhile the usual "soft soap" ceremony was performed. We were then dismissed to go about the camp as we pleased.

My first object was to hunt for food, and soon found lots of good flour and plenty of water, though not very sweet, with which I made some bannocks, which were soon baked, and very quickly eaten. Thus having appeased my voracious appetite, once more I strolled about the camp, and found the tent in which we left the aforesaid girl, who had been killed, I suppose, by some cold-blooded Sepoy, for the sake of her jewels, her remains being divested of the massive gold necklace, bracelets, earrings, and "'an innumerable quantity of finger rings, of gold, set with diamonds, and other precious stones, which she wore when we left her alive. I now regretted I had not asked her for a ring or two when my eyes were so dazzled with them; I am sure she would have given me any of them with pleasure.

These Seikhs have a strong penchant for bedizening their persons with costly ornaments—some of the higher classes wear them to the value of hundreds of pounds. I think it would tickle your fancy if you could see the "Knatch wallahs"* in this country, with numerous rings (not gold) on their toes, ankles, fingers, and arms, and in their noses and ears; with necklaces, and looking-glass rings, by the bye, on their thumbs, having their pretty faces coquettishly painted, and which only tends to disfigure their natural beauty. If I am allowed to be a judge, these are the handsomest girls I have ever seen in my travels, with all due deference to England's fair daughters, the gems of the world, whom I long to see, and will never leave again for foreign adventures.

I took a few yards of silk and two cashmere shawls out-of the tent to cover myself with during the night, which was fast approaching. I slept pretty well, and was tolerably warm and comfortable, being wrapped in silks.

Next morning (23rd) we struck the tents, and unlimbered all the guns we had captured. As four of our men were walking together they saw a Sepoy salaamming** the

* *Dancing Girls*
** *Worshipping*

cannon which we had taken from the enemy, this is expressive of their sympathy for the Seikhs; the soldiers debated for a minute whether to kill him or not, agreeing at last that he should live if all of them should miss him standing at about 200 yards off; which being settled, the result was his death from two bullets out of the four.

Around the camp we found several of the dead with their fingers cut partly and some wholly off apparently by the Sepoys, in order to get their gold rings, the bodies being so swollen that they could not be wrenched off without having recourse to the knife. All these Sepoys thought about was plundering the jewelry from the dead and wounded, and some of our men were tempted to do the same when there was no fighting going on.

Our duty called us to unlimber those guns winch made such devastation in the left division of our army, and more especially in the left wing of our regiment. Having so done we surveyed the dead that fell while storming this battery, and recognised many of them. 'Twas at this time I found the bodies of my Colonel and comrades before mentioned. What must be the feelings of my mind when thus beholding my brothers-in-arms lying dead around me, those whom romantic visions of glory had allured from the home of their parents; who resigned all the comforts and endearments of family and friends at the call of honour. No more shall they gladden the hearts of their fond relatives with tidings of their welfare; whose parents, alas! ignorant of their sudden end, cherished the fond hope of their return. They breathed their last afar from the abode of their infancy, without a friend to soothe their departure, or protect their wounded remains from the cold dews of that ever-memorable night.

The gallant and noble Prussian Prince, and his retinue of officers, fought with us in this great battle at Ferozeshuhur.

It is much lamented that his Surgeon, Doctor Hoffmeister, was killed in the action; he was seen to fall by His Royal Highness, who instantly sprang from his horse to the Doctor's assistance, with the hope that he was only wounded, but death had closed his career. The illustrious nobleman has now left our army and proceeded to Bombay, out of the Seikhs' grab.

The loss of the British in this ever-memorable engagement has been fearful, about 2500 are said to be killed and wounded.

Of our regiment Lieut.-Col. A.B. Taylor; Capt. J. Dunne and Capt. J. F. Field, killed. Major Barnwell; Capt, C. F Havelock, on the staff; Capt. A. Borton; Lieut. Cassidy; Lieut. Taylor; Lieut. Sievewright and Lieut. Vigors; Ensign Hanham and Ensign Foster, wounded. About 140 rank and file killed, and about 240 wounded, some but slightly, and others severely; and some died from their wounds in the hospitals at Ferozepore.

In this battle I believe our regiment's loss was greater than that of any in consequence of our storming and carrying the enemy's strongest position of defence on the 21st, soon after the commencement of the battle; but in the other two engagements we lost only a few men, I am happy to say, whilst many other regiments sustained great losses.

We now began to feel hungry again, which induced us to slaughter a few bullocks and goats we took from the enemy, from which each helped himself to a slice, and cooked it after his own fashion, eating it with bread that was brought to us by our Bubbagees★ from Moodkee; we likewise had a supply of liquor at the time which was very acceptable. I must tell you some part of our army found a profusion of liquor, wine, and other drinkables, in the camp, and got beastly drunk as two ammunition waggons, laden

★*Native Cooks*

with those drunken f—ls, were crossing an extensive powder mine, it exploded, blowing waggons, horses and men yards into the air. What do you think of that for a drunken spree? The enemy's camp was undermined with tons of gunpowder, and I very much marvel that our whole army was not blown to atoms when crossing and re-crossing it, as we carelessly did.

In the afternoon three mines exploded. Sentries were then placed over many others which the Sappers and Miners had discovered. It seems that about forty of the enemy, not valuing their lives a bit, came into the camp, disguised as villagers, with the design, doubtless, of springing the mines for our destruction; these fellows we soon found out, and shot most of them, and by way of example we pinioned and hung some on trees, teaching them to dance upon nothing, which I imagine is far more difficult and much less pleasing than the polka, which has lately been introduced into this country.

After this we marched about three miles from Ferozeshuhur to Sultan-Khan-Wallah in order to avoid the nauseous smell of many thousands of bodies in a state of decomposition, for by this time the whole atmosphere around seemed to be poisoned with the loathsome effluvia. At this place we captured two more of the Seikhs' guns in an easy manner, without firing a shot. Here we enjoyed a pretty comfortable night's rest, lying mend-the-muck-heap fashion.

Next day the wounded men's bedding came from Moodkee, and a party of us were sent with it to Ferozepore, a distance of about twelve miles, where several barracks were converted into hospitals. Who can describe the sufferings attendant on a military life ? we were soon in the midst of the harrowing scenes of an hospital. The sight of our suffering comrades, pining and languishing there, stimulated our already inflamed blood to the highest pitch, and we determined to have, as we subsequently had, *Revenge!* Whilst we were looking round the hospitals to find our more intimate companions, some were having bullets extracted from their bodies, some their arms and others their legs amputated; many died under the painful operations, but others, I am happy to say recovered, and are still living.

We returned to our regiment, and the next day, which was Christmas, we spent as merrily and as happily as you could expect, considering our situation, every one endeavouring to enliven each other. In the afternoon we had a "prayer" parade, after which the commanding officer read a proclamation to us, purporting that we should be presented with a medal, to decorate our breasts, for the valued services we had rendered our country in the fields of Moodkee and Ferozeshuhur.

Next day we marched to Bootawallah, about three miles off Sobraon, where our whole force encamped. Two days after a few men of every regiment were sent back on duty, with the Sappers and Miners; to spring all the powder mines at Ferozeshuhur; which amounted to nearly a hundred.

A few days afterwards we were reinforced by Her Majesty's 9th and 16th Lancers, and Her Majesty's 10th and 53rd regiments of Infantry with all the heavy ordnance from the interior of Bengal, which comprised elephant and bullock batteries, and all the siege train; also a vast number of Native Artillery, Cavalry and Infantry, altogether making our force immensely strong.

At the same time Major-G.-L. Davis of our regiment, who had been on detachment, joined us, and took command of the regiment, and was soon appointed Colonel. Promotions amongst the officers were rapid in this campaign in consequence of the numbers killed in the two battles.

Shortly after Sir Harry Smith took the smaller part of our force to Aliwal, and there gave a division of the Seikh army a good drubbing; in which I understood the 16th Lancers signalized themselves by their unexampled courage and intrepidity; they fought not only bravely but most desperately. The lances could not possible be wielded with more dexterity, or with better aim, or produce greater effects than on that brilliant occasion. The enemy lost about 8000 and the British only about 400, which clearly shows what we could do with the Seikhs, were they not screened by strong fortifications, constructed by Europeans, with skill and military judgment.

The 16th Lancers are the finest set of men I have ever seen out of London. During the engagement at Aliwal we were still at Bootawallah, watching the Seikh grand army at Sobraon. Here Sir Hugh Gough was indefatigable in his duty; I have seen him riding about at all times in the night watching the enemy's motions with his night glass.

In this position we remained a long time, living like fighting-cocks, on the best of provisions that could be procured in this locality. We endeavoured to amuse ourselves with playing cards, and various other games, which tended to dispel the gloomy thoughts arising from such fearful tragedies as we had lately witnessed. It is a very superstitious idea I admit, but I have a forcible impression that a man prior to his going into the field of action has a presentiment of his fate; for instance, I have known on such occasions the most inveterate gamblers in our regiment all at once lose their ardour in the pursuit of it, at the same time looking very dejected, and would shake hands with their comrades, having a conviction that it was for the last time—these men had a strong impression of soon being killed. Having written letters for some of them, they would have bequeathed me their effects, but I would not accept them under such a pretence; it is no more singular than true that these soldiers actually were killed.

One morning, while suffering the most excruciating pain from a tooth, we were ordered to turn out in fighting order. I hurried on my accoutrements, and having seized my firelock, ran almost frantic to our apothecary to have it extracted; the dentist, however, could not find his instruments, but gave me a small piece of lint soaked with a stinging hot liquid to apply to my tooth instead. I remarked in leaving him that the Seikhs might possibly knock it out for me. I ran and fell in with my regiment, and soon after the pain left me.

We marched some distance from camp and took up a position on the defensive at the same time our Artillery fired a few shots, merely to take the range, but the Cavalry and Infantry did nothing, only the looking-on part.

We sallied out several times prepared for battle, and returned without accomplishing our design. About half-way between our camp and the enemy's there was a small fort which we took possession of for a look-out post, where we could better, and with more safety, watch the Seikhs' motions at Sobraon. A small body of our men were sent to this look-out post every morning, and returned at night.

It came to my turn to go once, and when there on duty we could just see the enemy's camp, from whence some of them came within range of our musket shot to cut grass for their horses; we did not allow them forage so close to us unmolested, but shot several of these grass-cutters. This was a daily custom, until one morning a guard went as usual and to their surprise found the enemy occupying the fort. Our Sappers and Miners had been several days employed in excavating entrenchments within distance range of the enemy's shot, for a lookout post; this being completed, our regiment and two regiments of Sepoys, with an adequate proportion of Artillery, were detached from the main army to occupy these works. Sentinels of Cavalry were posted between us and the mainforce, so that if the enemy advanced we could soon apprize the whole army of our danger, and being fenced in by breast-works, could keep the marauders at bay till other troops came to our assistance; but we were not molested.

While we were in this camp the enemy came reconnoitering so close that we shot several of them. Our duty was somewhat fatigueing in this position; I was myself on outlying picket every alternate night. Outlying picket means that a strong guard quits the entrenchments at dusk in the evening, and advances near the enemy's night watch, having a double chain of sentries planted at distances communicating with each other, whose duty it is to fire and retire, should any one approach, and at day-break in the morning to return to camp.

On February 9th, 1846, at night, we received orders to prepare for action next morning, which caused a general excitement among our troops. Artillery, Cavalry, and Infantry were all in a state of exhilaration, taking up the most advantageous positions. Early in the morning, before the enemy's picket withdrew, a regiment of Ghoorkahs, in our service, took them by surprise, and destroyed the whole of them with their choorahs.* It seems that they (the enemy's picket) were not watching with vigilance, as was their duty, but were sleeping, though probably not dreaming of their fearful end.

These Ghoorkahs are a very diminutive race of men, but decidedly the best Day and Martin soldiers in India, boasting they are an arm's length better soldiers than any other native tribes in the country, and that we are the same

* *Large Knives*

length better than they. We celebrated the anniversary of Her Gracious Majesty's wedding day (February 10th) by firing a *feu de joie*. At the dawn of day having every thing definitely arranged to give battle, our Artillery poured a volley of shells and rockets into the enemy's camp, arousing them from their slumber, and on their not retaliating, we thought they were decamping; but soon, however, they got their guns to bear upon us, though happily their aim was bad, for most part of their shells burst in the air, and the long shots all bounded over the ravines in which we (Infantry) were sheltered.

We now made the Seikhs feel the full weight of our wrath; our rockets in particular did great execution, spreading fearful terror and destruction amongst them. After some splendid cannonading for about three hours, the Infantry advanced, when our regiment, being in the rear, forming the reserve, we had a very beautiful view of the attack; what a magnificent sight to be sure! I shall never forget it.

Her Majesty's 10th regiment was in front of us, and most of their men threw aside their heavy shakos (caps) and went in a perisher! (as we term it) with the Seikhs; it was quite a novelty to them as their regiment was never before engaged in battle; they came to close quarters and were repulsed, but when they saw our brigade advancing, they renewed the attack and drove back the enemy, but not without a great sacrifice of men, for the slaughter here was terrible.

It was there Sir Robert Dick was killed, a brave veteran and Waterloo officer, whose loss was deeply lamented by all his regiment.

At another part of the camp Her Majesty's 29th was repulsed three times, and the enemy's Cavalry charged them, and out off 29 men's heads, before our horsemen could get to their assistance; we afterwards placed the bodies in a row, and remarked that it was singular enough, the number of the regiment should exactly correspond with the 29 decapitated fellows who lay before us. The 3rd Dragoons here made a brilliant charge, while we were advancing, and chopped the Seikhs down at a tremendous rate.

In a foregoing page I mentioned Lieutenant Creagh; as our brigade was advancing in line towards the scene of action, this officer in charge of my company was marching in the ordinary manner, a man on either side of him, when instinctively he suddenly bowed himself down and the next moment a cannon ball passed right over him, and went smashing through a drum head which a boy was carrying. Had this not been the case at the moment, he would certainly have been struck in the chest.

While advancing we were all at once alarmed at seeing in front of us, to the right, one of our ammunition waggons in a blaze, and the poor frightened horses urged on by the fierce flame behind them, galloping in full speed towards the enemy's camp, the battle at the same time raging on all sides.

I think it was about nine o'clock that our Artillery ceased firing, then we (Infantry) and all the Cavalry attacked the Seikhs with bright steel, which they cannot stand; we slaughtered thousands in the camp, and thousands that escaped the sword and bayonet, were either shot or drowned while crossing the river Sutlej, as their bridge had been previously destroyed by our Artillery's fire. There was a battery of guns on the other side of the river, which made great havoc in our ranks, and these the enemy bore away in their flight.

We were an equal match for the foe at Sobraon, having our army reinforced, whilst theirs was reduced; notwithstanding, they then had the superiority, besides the advantage of an entrenched camp, defended by about 36,000 men and 70 bulldogs; (great guns) and having a double row of half-moon batteries—high ramparts, with immense deep and wide ditches—a triple line of defences of earth and planks, with facines, redoubts, and epaulments.

You see the camp was as inaccessible as a formidable fort; the Seikhs were determined we should not run in upon them and take their guns this time without great difficulty. The battle was nearly over when our brigade entered their camp at one end, and got in the rear of their strongest position, but we found ourselves between two fires—from a battery on the other side of the Sutlej on our left, and from the remnant of their Infantry and Artillery on the right; but happily for us their exertions had little or no effect. Soon the enemy yielded, offering no further resistance, and I really could not help feeling for their Infantry, at seeing them marching away so deliberately with trailed arms—offering no return whatever to our galling fire; and as they got out of our reach, fell victims to our more advanced troops, which extended as far as the river's bank.

You have, doubtless, read of the "red sea;" and the Sutlej now might very well be called the "red river" from the blood of thousands of the Seikhs, many of whose bodies are floating down the river at this time.

After the battle we found amongst the fallen a true patriot of theirs, a wooden-legged Seikh, who was severely wounded, but we did not kill him; we found several others in the same state, whose lives we preserved; but some effective and armed Seikhs we killed without any compunction whatever; yet how revolting to see these poor victims lay before us in such intense agony—struggling on their backs—with the hemorrhage gushing from a bayonet prick in the heart—their flashing eyes rolling most frightfully, and menacingly staring us in the face. Never did Van Hamburgh's eyes look so fierce while performing with his wild beasts. The number of the enemy killed in this our most glorious and decisive battle is computed at 12,000, and those which we did not destroy, ran away, and may be running till this time for what I know or care. We piled arms and buried all the European dead; the wounded were conveyed to camp, and from thence to the hospitals at Ferozepore. Having been complimented as usual with the *soft soap* ceremony, we returned to our camp, and whilst marching from the battle field and after we had arrived, the prevalent topic and opinion was, that the enemy had now played their last game with us.

> *"With all our force's strength and might,*
> *We put the treach'rous foe to flight;*
> *This morning, ere the break of day,*
> *In silence we all marched away,*
> *And took our station m the field,*
> *Then rockets at the Seikhs to wield,*
> *(The fiery sticks by them so term'd,)*
> *Soon made them very much alarm'd;*
> *Our shells too, played their part we know,*
> *And many hundreds they laid low;*
> *Some smaller pills the Seikhs got then,*
> *Which chok'd some hundreds of their men ;*
> *Our swordmen next assailed the Seikhs,*
> *Regarding not their dreadful shrieks ;*
> *Our gleaming bay'nets next they saw,*
> *Which made them dread us more and more;*
> *When all these weapons got to play,*
> *The Seikhs recoil'd and ran away,*
> *But would not yield till they were forc'd,*
> *Though thousands in the field they lost;*
> *We now return with vict'ry crown'd,*

And leave the dying souls around;
To night we rest from thought and care,
No murd'rous hand have we to fear;
Unlike the weary nights we've passed,
'Mid dangers since December last;
Our swords and bay'nets sheath'd once more,
We sing hurrah ! the war is o'er."

Ever since I have been in the army, I have found it a great inconvenience that my name begins with a "B," as we are alphabetically enrolled "A," "B," "C," and so forth, and whenever there be any extra duty to do, however objection- able it may be, it always devolves on the parties whose names stand first on the roll.

Next morning (11th) six men of each company of our regiment, myself one as a matter of course, were sent on duty to the battle field, to bring all the guns (67 in number) which we had captured, to our camp, it being the nearest to Sobraon.

When we got there, we had the curiosity, to examine the redoubts and trenches, which were nearly filled with dead Seikhs, all of whom were denuded of their clothing by fire, and their bodies horribly burnt. I remarked to my comrades at the time, (as the thought struck me,) that those poor fellows must have had a presentiment of their fate, and not liking the idea of lying about the field like so many rotten sheep, and becoming a prey to the vultures and wild beasts, which are very numerous in this locality, made graves for themselves to ensure their being buried. The most fearful carnage was presented here, upwards of 15,000 dead bodies, the result of a few hours bloody contest. I trust never to see so horrible a sight again.

Here we experienced a wonderful instance of the all-merciful hand of providence in guiding and protecting our party from an awful death; for had we not loitered about in surveying the dead, and been tardy in the execution of our duty we should inevitably have been on the face of an extensive powder mine, which exploded within about sixty yards, immediately in front of us, making the earth tremble beneath our feet, and presenting an indescribable scene; many (though happily already dead) bodies and a quantity of earth floating in the air, amidst enormous masses of smoke and flames. We returned with the guns to our camp, where we remained in quiet for two days; our whole force then crossed the Sutlej and cautiously proceeded towards Lahore, the capital of the Punjaub. In our route we had to ford a very broad stream, about three feet deep: some of our men stripped and waded through it, but others, with myself, crossed over with our clothes on; our bigger men volunteered to carry their favourite serjeants across; one in particular took off his belts and gave them with his musket to a very old color-serjeant, whom he undertook to carry: it was quite laughable to see the old man mounted on his shoulders, and still more so when they got to the deepest part, about half way across, where the current was very strong, so that the bearer lost his footing, thus immersing the old fellow over head and ears, in the middle of the river, with both their fire-locks and accoutrements; I could not forbear laughing at this circumstance, although it reminded me of being awkwardly situated, in somewhat similar circumstances myself.

In my first campaign, marching up the country as a raw recruit, without arms and accoutrements, I often had to ford streams and rivulets, but I never once stripped, nor even so much as took off my boots, lest I should be bitten by water snakes or cut my feet. I did not then, however, much mind walking in wet clothes, as I usually had plenty of brandy in a tin flask, which I carried to bathe both within and outside; I always liked to have a dry bed to lie in; and which was conveyed from one camp ground to another, on hackarahs;* one morning as some I of these were going through a larger river than usual, I saw the greater part of the low cart under water, and most of the beds; my own happening to come up at the time, I took it, with the anticipation of carrying it across dry, on my shoulder, but when I came to the middle of the stream, I was raised up by the force of the current and my bed dropped into the water. How delightful! I had thought it a wise trick to carry mine, after seeing others getting wet, so I tried my wisdom for once, and you see what I gained by it; however, I persevered in towing my saturated bed ashore, and making another with handkerchiefs, &c., to serve while it was getting dry, which it soon did under the scorching rays of an Indian sun.

Soldiers in this country often meet with many inconveniences and much trouble, independent of the battle field and hard fighting.

During the march some of the Seikh chiefs met our political agents and proposed the outlines of a treaty of peace; and one day His Highness the Maharajah Dhuleep Singh, quite a boy, and the Ranee** visited our camp.

A few days' tedious marching in the enemy's country, brought us to the city, but the Lahorian government had agreed to our terms rather than we should demolish their town.' Our Governor-General and Commander-in-Chief having arrived at a very good understanding with the Lahorian crown, we encamped about two miles off Lahore, where I am spending some of the happiest days of my so-

* Indian carts, drawn by bullocks of the buffalo species
** Queen and Sovereign of the nation

journ in this country. One day we had a superlative grand parade, in reviewing order, on this extensive plain, about 50,000 of us, and when each regiment's band played, I assure you it almost turned me giddy with delight. What a striking contrast was this, from the fearful and hideous noise of battle, to the exhilarating sounds of music, sweet, sweet music,

> "*Whose sounds the fiercest grief can charm,*
> *And fate's severest rage disarm!*
> *Sweet music softens pain to ease,*
> *And makes despair and madness please ;*
> *Our joys below it doth improve,*
> *And antedates the bliss above.*"

At this review I had the opportunity of seeing Sir Charles Napier, a very able general and brave soldier, the gallant conqueror of Scinde, and the terror of that country, who is called, by the Seikhs, Sheitanka Bhaee;* he had come with his force from the Scinde country to our aid and support, but we had accomplished the work, and needed not his assistance. Sir Charles is not unlike a Seikh to look at; his complexion is dark, with much hair on his face.

I suppose when if ever, I come back to the land of my nativity, I must bring with me two witnesses to prove my identity, being so much altered in appearance; besides, I must tell you I have climbed up in the world since I saw you, tall enough to stand in the front rank.

I have often, of late, been in company with Pratt, Plum, and Brownsell, from Swaffham, whom you know right well; they are in Her Majesty's 10th foot: were in the last engagement with me, and fortunate enough to escape unscathed.

Pratt, Brownsell, and myself were invulnerable; Plum was slightly wounded, but not disabled much, as he continued

---

*The devil's brother

with his regiment all through, the piece. I told them I was writing to you an account of the sport we have had together so far from home, and they desired me to present their respects, and request you to see their families and friends at Swaffham, and tell them they are still living after taking part in one battle. (Sobraon.) I also beg you will make my kindest remembrances to them and all inquiring friends. I imagine that some of my old cronies are for ever asking if you have not heard from the "Wild Russian," for I fancy they often talk about me and the "Wild Antelope." Is it not very remarkable that we two wild young fellows should both enlist the same month, and meet here in battle together. You know I was called the " Wild Russian," and Pratt the "Wild Antelope," at Swaffham; when I first recognised Pratt in soldiers equipage amongst a number of other recruits on Chatham parade ground, I made him stare by exclaiming "Antelope."

You know elephants are tamed in this country, so you may readily imagine that we are by this time, somewhat tractable, having now pretty well "sown our wild oats."

I will now introduce to you my constant and sincere friend, Dick Wilson, from the Emerald Isle, a nice fellow; he called me one day when I was busy writing, to take a stroll with him; we went all round the walls of Lahore, which are about four miles and a half in circumference, and concurred in opinion that there would have been an enormous sacrifice of life if we had had to besiege this strongly fortified town, with batteries and sally-ports all round it.

Being armed with two tolerably sized sticks, we ventured to go and glance at the interior of the city, which is a miserable dirty sinkhole of a place, we were very much disappointed with it, so would any one judging from its exterior. The citizens paid us as much homage as if we had been kings, but we doubted their sincerity, knowing they undoubtedly would rather not have seen us there; they received, however, the greatest courtesy from us. We passed through what we call "the lall bazaar," a seraglio to the extent of a whole street, in which were confined nearly all the beauties of the metropolis; there were many groups of these girls squinting at us from windows on both sides; it reminded me somewhat of ladies in England looking down from windows and balconies at a procession in the street on some particular occasion.

We eventually came to the royal palaces, where we met some soldier-like men on sentry, wearing gold medals, distinguishing badges of honour, for their services under the crown. Here we were greatly at a loss, not knowing their language, all we understood from these officers was Ranee, a host of Rajahs, Maharajahs, and Singhs; as for what else they said, it might be calling us all sorts of opprobrious names, we could not tell.

The residences of the royal family are not by far such elegant buildings as I have seen in other parts of India; there were a few in a very dilapidated state, which I have no doubt were once very splendid. It is a singular custom with the natives to build in a most magnificent style, but when they decay a little, never to repair them, but let them fall to ruin.

Our being the first soldiers that had been in Lahore, and having returned without molestation, we related our adventures to our comrades, and several of them were induced to visit the city.

Having brought to your notice R.W., I have another intimate friend, Stephen Hovee, from Aylsham, whose parents our people at Felmingham know quite well. I have one of the best of chums, Charley Beard, who attends to me when I am on duty, and carefully sees after all my things during my absence; in return I do the same for him. Should I not live to see you, and you ever happen to meet either of these men, at any future time, remember me, and treat them well, as I have the greatest respect for them.

At the signing of the treaty here, I beheld a very rich procession of the Seikh royalty, but not by any means so grand as the procession of our Royal Family, which I once saw in London, notwithstanding the Seikhs riding (in gold and silver houdahs★) on their elephants; all the the elephants and horses in the procession were richly caparisoned.

While the articles were being read, the Seikh grandees sat on solid gold chairs, each of which, I understood, took four men to carry. I am almost surprised that these people themselves are not made of gold and silver. However, I think the British will reap a golden harvest here, and we all shall soon wear gold and silver buttons; in fact some of us do already. I cannot refrain from expressing my admiration of the Seikhs' household troops; two complete regiments of boys, (foot,) a troop of horse-boys, and a few small, but splendid, pieces of cannon, which, as Paddy says, were manned by boys.

Respecting the treaty between us and them, they were constrained by it, to surrender a great tract of territory, which is very fertile land, and will realize an immense tribute; and pay £1,500,000 sterling, as an indemnity for the expenses of the war; to disband their present army and re-organise one on the system and regulations with regard to pay, as in the time of the late Maharajah Bunjeet Singh, and to surrender all those guns which were pointed against us, that we did not capture.

I must now tell you that about 250 pieces of heavy cannon, about 40,000 muskets and matchlocks, about 30,000 swords and various other deadly weapons, were not, after all, sufficient to kill me, I am happy to say.

★ *A large chair for four persons to sit in, fastened on an elephant's back*

Why the Seikhs are so formidable in battle is, that they have been trained and drilled by European officers, English, Irish, Scotch, French, Spanish, and Dutch.

Also their strongholds, with redoubts, fascines, epaulments, and so forth, are planned and constructed by first rate European engineers; and their mode of attack drawn out by European generals. The Seikhs are exceedingly well disciplined by these officers, and would fight us at a respectful distance for everlasting. But these officers, with all their eminent skill, could not impart to them the courage of true Englishmen. They will fight bravely till tested with never-failing steel, then when death stares them in the face, their courage fails. I have heard that the Seikhs should say, they would now fight us, if we fought fairly and honestly, not steal from them their guns, which was our principal aim, and you perceive we succeeded, but not without the price of much bloodshed. I maintain that we have been fighting all this time against foreign skill and assistance; for we found amongst the slain, several Europeans. The joy of his family—pride of North "Walsham—star of Norfolk—glory and saviour of England—terror of France—hero and baron of the Nile—Duke of Bronte and victim of Trafalgar—the famous Nelson, during his memorable life and brilliant career, once remarked that "one Englishman was equal to three Frenchmen." Being myself from Norfolk and. having the honour of serving in its own regiment, I beg leave to say that an Englishman is equivalent to eight Seikhs, as you will perceive by 'their loss in this war, which has been about 60,000, while ours, I am happy to say, is not 8000.

We often see Tej Singh and a whole host of the Singh family; these chiefs and all the princes and nobles in this country, are a most licentious people; revelling and luxuriating in every voluptuous and sensual pleasure that the most depraved imagination can possibly conceive. The Ranee, too, we have seen, who is now past the bloom and vigour of life; although queen-like, with much dignity, she has hitherto exercised no moral restraint over her passions and innate depravity, so common in oriental women, but gives herself up to the debasing influence of a corrupt mind. I do not wish to dilate upon this subject, but simply to acknowledge, and with great pleasure too, that they have been very kind and liberal to our army since we have been here, presenting us with scores of sheep. They have great antipathy to our killing bullocks, saying it is defiling their sacred and holy land; but it has been told them the English are all real beef-eaters. It is a remarkable fact, that they do not half so much mind our having killed thousands of their men, as they do our killing and eating beef in their country; they seem to shudder at the very thoughts of it.

It seems the occasion of this fierce and bloody war was, that the Seikhs, without any provocation whatever from the British, selected a part of the country where there are no practicable roads, and stealthily invaded our territories, with the avowed intention of exterminating all the Europeans in India, and making slaves of the women.

But, however, we frustrated their base designs, and may God bless and ever protect our fair and beautiful creatures from such brutes as the Seikhs. Thus you perceive, in this war we fought on the defensive, to retain what we already had in our possession; we were not infringing on the Seikhs' territories, and, I am happy to say, that this has been the most justifiable and successful struggle the British ever had in this country. In reference to the Afghanistan war, the British, in the first place, had no right to interfere whatever; secondly, they sacrificed thousands of lives to no good purpose whatever, and in the third place, they were left minus by thousands and thousands of pounds. Methinks I hear you exclaim, what business have we in this country at all?

I am sure I am unprepared to answer you, as I profess to handle the battle axe, not the political hatchet. I suppose it is that sword and might overcome right. We laugh and say sometimes, that we come here as saints, for the purpose of converting the heathen Indians.

> *"If we've not converted any,*
> *Lately we've subverted many."*

Alluding to those two men in a foregoing page, who did not much admire war at first, I have the great pleasure and satisfaction to say, in extenuation of their misconduct at Moodkee, that they stood the brunt of the last two battles, I believe, pretty well; and as I wish to be charitable to my neighbours, I feel it my duty to urge this in their defence.

I have now to relate a very amusing story of a true Irishman: the day prior to the battle of Sobraon, the orderly Serjeant warned Matthew (his name) for duty next day; but as we assailed the enemy the same morning,, the old guard kept on duty till after the engagement; when the new guard therefore paraded, and as usual were inspected by the Serjeant-Major, he, on examining their arms, found "Matthew's was quite clean; this is very strange, thought the Serjeant-Major, and he asked Matthew how his firelock came to be so bright at such a time, unlike the others, saying, " did you not fire at all during the action." Matthew replied, " Fait Surrah de Saarjint tould me yistherday I vos for garrud this murning, so o coorse I claaned me firelock, an I dint like to durrty it firring at dose Seikhs, dere vos enow to do dat widout me." The Serjeant-Major thought the best way would be to pass it over with a hearty laugh, in which we all joined. You see we have some curious creatures, indeed almost f—ls, in the army; a man is not a soldier for the strength and soundness of his intellect, but for his indomitable bravery and discipline, perfect soundness and healthiness of body, of which the medical officers are very particular, in their examination. If soldiers were not a most hardy set of fellows, they could not possibly endure the various changes of climate, the fatigues of campaigning, and the harassing duties of warfare to which they are liable during their service.

At Astley's amphitheatre, in London, I once saw performed "the battle of Waterloo," which was altogether so stimulating to a young and uncultivated yet enterprising mind like mine, that it had a striking tendency to fire my zeal for a soldier's life, which I now experience to my heart's desire, having performed my part in a battle which I might term "the Waterloo of India." But now the war is over and peace proclaimed, I can laugh and sing God save the Queen, my country and the army; which was sang, and elicited great applause, at Swaffham, on the Queen's wedding day. You remember the man who sang it got the prize.

I conclude with a feeling of affection for you and all my relatives, to whom, perhaps, you will consign this narrative in their turns, and who will, I trust, not think me egotistical in thus presenting them and you with the results of my own personal observations and adventures during my military career, since I last wrote to you, showing the natural propensity which I always felt for a roving and adventurous life. You know I had no rest at home, I was always desirous of visiting foreign countries; I have now had a good slice of it, and feel quite satisfied.

But my race is not yet run; we expect to march in a few days to our future quarters at Meerut, which is about 400 miles from this place; we shall then have nearly 1000 miles more to march down the country at some future time, if peace continues; and in the event of another war breaking out, heaven knows how many hundreds of miles we may yet have to travel. It is now rumoured that there are a few rebellious chiefs in the lower provinces agitating, and there is not a shadow of doubt, had our army been defeated by the Seikhs, all the natives throughout the land would have revolted against the British.

I hope and believe that nothing will be found incorrect throughout this narrative of the last four months of my life, but I felt irresistibly urged to introduce some parts of a peculiar and melancholy cast, and some of the most gloomy and heartrending scenes which occurred. I think you will not read unmoved some of these touching facts. I am only a solitary unit in what I have endeavoured to describe; there were thousands who felt the same deep sympathy as myself, and thousands, of the bravest men have laid down their lives for their country. Some persons have said "it is sweet to die for one's country," but I am not quite sure of that; I think it sweeter far to live, what say you?

I hope I shall not trespass too much on your time, and on that of my other friends, by your perusal of this short narrative when you receive it completed. I do not send it to you as a literary production and highly varnished; quite the contrary, a simple history of facts, which sometimes, however, are stranger than fiction; you will be quite ready to excuse any error or imperfection in the style and composition when I tell you that I have been several days writing amidst continued interruptions from my comrades, and fancy my having the ground for a floor, and lying on it, with my knapsack and portfolio across my knees.

Though I am your senior in years, yet I suppose I must not presume to hint that you will find a piece or two of good advice in this narrative. And if you know a second or third volume of a "Wild Russian or Antelope," I think their reading and digesting this would not be at all amiss. Be pleased to make my kindest regards to my old companions and friends at Swaffham. Now adieu; and that health, happiness, and long life may continue to be your portion, is the sincere prayer of your once roving, but now wiser Cousin,

J. W. Baldwin

P.S. You know I am a wretched singer, but at any rate I will now give you a song—Regimental—Tune, "Rule Britannia;" words by myself.

The gallant old ninth fresh glory has seen,
Thus fighting abroad for our country and Queen;
The county of Norfolk will pride in its corps,
When hearing our feats with the troops of Lahore.

Chorus—Rule Britannia, &c.

Come now, my brave comrades, let's hasten to claim
The honours that we gain'd in the three fields of fams,
Britannia has triumphed on the plains of Moodkee,
Where her sons, for the first time, made the proud Seikhs to flee.

Chorus—Rule Britannia, &c.

Come sound your trumpets, brave conquerors sound,
The foes of our country are dying around;
Jehovah has fought for the British once more,
For in triumph we marched from the field of Ferozeshuhur.

Chorus—Rule Britannia, &c.

The Seikhs had assembled their forces at length,
And bade defiance to the British strength;
The 10th of February, on the plains of Sobraon,
We killed thousands of the foe, and the victory won.

Chorus—Rule Britannia, &c.

But whilst we rejoice in the victories won
Remember our comrades that are now dead and gone,
Who rushed at the enemy, by our sides we all know,
And fell by the hands of the treacherous foe.

Chorus—Rule Britannia, &c.

Who could, then, despise the soldiers brave,
Who volunteered to fight, their country to save,
But rather respect them, for their duty they've done
In the field at Moodkee, Ferozeshuhur, and Sobraon.

Chorus—Rule Britannia, &c.

THE END

A History of the Sutlej Campaign
December 1845 – March 1846

In the following brief history of the Sutlej Campaign passages that relate directly to the activities of H. M. 9th Foot in the first section of this book have been printed in bolder type to assist the reader in identifying those events which bear directly on Baldwin's experiences.

Opening of the Campaign
December

On the 13th December Sir Henry Hardinge received the intelligence that the body of the Sikh army had crossed the Sutlej on the 11th; and then issued the proclamation which was the virtual Decleration of War.

The crossing of the Sutlej by the Sikhs continued an act of war, and opened the Sutlej Campaign. The narrative here set forth is almost exclusively military; and it is to military details that our attention must now be turned.

Information as to the Sikh army is not quite as precise as might be desired. But there are certain facts with regard to it which are quite definitely known.

It was under the leadership of Tej Singh, a Sikh Sirdar of some position and repute, who was probably in touch with the Court party, and certainly believed that nothing but disaster would come of the war. Associated with him in the leadership was Rajah Lall Singh, the favourite of the Rani Jindan, and nominal Vizier. It must, however, be observed that there is no evidence in proport of the assertion which has been made that these chiefs were guilty of treachery.

The army itself was filled with a vehemently hostile feeling towards the British, and a strong sense of self-confidence and of loyalty to the Khalsa. Loyalty to the Durbar it had none; its vows were to the Sikh brotherhood, very much as our Covenanters gave their allegiance to the Covenant. But this turbulent and insubordinate body, recklessly democratic in its political, treatment of the Government, was fully alive to the impossibility of democratic methods in the field; and the Panchayets now laid aside their assumed control, formally accepting the purely military organisation for purely military purposes.

The component parts of the regular army had been wholly reorganized by Ranjit Singh. In the old days the vast bulk of the Sikhs had been horsemen; infantry and artillery were condemned or misunderstood. Ranjit Singh, not without valuable help from his European officers – Allard, Ventura, Avitabile, and others - had educated his people into preferring the infantry to the cavalry service, and into becoming first-class artillerymen. Consequently, in 1845, the regular army was composed somewhat as follows: artillery, which could bring 200 guns into the field and serve them admirably; 35 foot regiments of 1000 men each; and 15,000 cavalry, known as "Ghorchurras." But in addition to these regulars, who, when it came to fighting, showed splendid discipline, an immense force could be brought into action, consisting of the private levies of the Sirdars. Neither in armament nor in discipline were these men at all on a level with the regular army, but both in infantry and cavalry they are estimated have numbered nearly double of the trained troops.

According to information received by Major Broadfoot late in November, the plan of the Lahore Durbar was to send five out of the seven divisions of the regulars against the British. Allowing for the artillery, this would seem to mean a body of from 40,000 to 50,000 men. If the Sirdar's contingents be added to these, it is probable that the whole Sikh force destined to do battle with the British troops did not fall short of 100,000. No such force, however, was ever collected at one time against the British. It should, perhaps, be noted that Captain Cunningham, in his "History of the Sikhs," places the numbers very much lower. It is not, indeed, clear from his narrative how numerous he reckoned the Sikh army which crossed the Sutlej to have been; but he seems to put it at between 30,000 and 40,000 regulars, with half the number of irregulars. While giving due weight to his opinion, however, it must be remembered that he wrote always as an enthusiastic admirer of the Sikhs, with a strong inclination to give the benefit of every doubt in their favour.

As regards our own troops, the reader to-day should perhaps be reminded that in the year 1845 the British army in India was armed entirely with the old "Brown Bess" of the Peninsular War, the fire of which was not effective much beyond 300 yards, disciplined troops rarely firing a shot till within half that distance from the enemy. The effective range of field artillery was about 800 yards for round shot and shell; about 300 for "grape". The Sikh artillery was as good as our own; their guns were more numerous; and the infantry muskets were the same as ours.

In order to follow the movements of the armies with any accuracy, it will now be necessary to give considerable attention to the map of the "theatre of the war".

It will be obvious that the first objective of the force invading from Lahore would be Ferozepore, in the immediate neighbourhood of the point on the Sutlej where the troops would naturally cross.

Ferozepore, as will readily be seen, was the most advanced of the British military stations, being the western-most post on the Sutlej. Here, and at Ludhiana, also very near the Sutlej, 80 miles to the east of Ferozepore, Sir Henry Hardinge, the Governor-General, and Sir Hugh Gough, the Commander-in-Chief, had throughout 1845 been steadily and quietly increasing the garrisons; also a large number of boats adapted for building pontoons had been collected.

Ferozepore itself was an open cantonment, without any attempt at fortification; though in view of the threatening attitude of the Sikh army, Major-General Sir John Littler, an experienced and trustworthy officer who commanded, had thrown up some shelter trenches and light field works to aid in the defence. It was garrisoned by two troops of Horse Artillery, and two light field batteries of 6 guns each; H.M.'s 62nd Foot, the 12th, 14th, 27th, 33rd, 44th, 54th and 63rd Regiments Native Infantry; the 8th Native Light Cavalry, and the 3rd Irregulars - numbering altogether about 7000 fighting men, taking the infantry regiments at 700 and the cavalry at 300.

The composition of the force was, as can be seen, almost entirely native - a great disadvantage, considering its very exposed position; but as there was no barrack accommodation for another British regiment the reinforcement had been postponed. At Ludhiana, about 80 miles almost due east of Ferozepore, also on the banks of the Sutlej which was about 10 miles distant, there was a small fort. It was held by a force under Brigadier H. M. Wheeler, at that time a very able and reliable officer (subsequenlty so unhappily connected with the great Cawnpore disaster in 1857), consisting of H.M.'s 50th Foot, the 11th, 26th, 42nd, 48th and 73rd Regiments Native Infantry, one regiment Native Cavalry and two troops Horse Artillery - about 5000 fighting men, with 12 guns.

These two cantonments were situated within the Sikh Protected States.

Umballa, the principal station in support of the two advanced posts, was about 80 miles from Ludhiana and 160 from Ferozepore by the most direct routes. The country between was a dead flat, very sandy and dusty; the road being mere tracks and extremely heavy either to march over or for carts, but better suited for camels, which were principally used by the people. There were very few villages and little or no water except from wells dug by the villagers; while, for the most part, the country was overgrown with camel-thorn and low jungle trees without any undergrowth - a very different country to what it is now.

Umballa was held by a fairly strong garrison under a most able and gallant soldier, Major-General Walter Raleigh Gilbert. It consisted of H.M.'s 9th, 31st and 80th Regiments of Infantry; The 16th, 24th, 41st, 45th and 47th Regiments of Native Infantry; the 3rd Light Dragoons, 4th and 5th Regiments Light Cavalry and the Governor-General's body-guard formed the cavalry; and, in addition to these, there were the 29th Foot at Kassauli, and the 1st Bengal European Regiment at Subathu, both in the hills. This whole force would amount to about 10,000 fighting men, good men and true, efficient and fit for anything, and held ready to move, literally, at a moment's notice.

These troops – Ferozepore, 7000; Ludhiana, 5000; Umballa, with Kassauli and Subathu, 10.000 – were all that were available to meet any sudden emergency; for Meerut, the next large station – too far off to appear in the map – was about 130 miles by road, nor could large bodies of troops be put in motion, equipped for a campaign, without some delay. A certain amount of transport was kept up ready for immediate use at each station, but beyond that transport animals, mostly camels had to be requisitioned or got in by civil authorities.

The commissariat Department, though it may have worked expensively, was, however, very efficient, and supplies of all sorts were generally fully and rapidly obtained.

At Meerut there was a force of about 9000 men and 26 guns, viz. 9th and 16th Lancers, 3rd Light Cavalry, H.M.'s 10th, Foot (save one company), the corps of sappers and miners, and several regiments of native infantry, which could be pushed forward in support, and might come into the field later on.

There were also two Goorkha regiments, the Nusseeree Battalion near Simla, and the Sirmoor Battalion at Deyrah Dhoon which were available at a comparatively short notice.

The backbone of the Indian army consisted of the British troops; but, unfortunately, there were very few of them, and too-much reliance was placed in those days on the sepoys. These on the whole, did well, sometimes very well, led by British officers, and encouraged by the presence and example of the British regiments. Sir Henry Hardinge considered that they-were about on a par with the Portuguese troops, with whom he had served during the Peninsular War, and that, like them, they had their "fighting" days. But they were not made of the same stuff as Englishmen; and this was well known to the Sikhs, who invariably concentrated their fire and attention on the English regiments, feeling confident that if they could only stop them the others would soon give way.

Sir Hugh Gough, the Commander-in-chief, had been fully alive to the insecurity of Ferozepore, situated as it was within, such easy striking distance of the Sikh frontier, and so far from all support. Being responsible for the military safety of the frontier, he earnestly wished to take all precautionary measures to meet the possible contingency of a war, and to bring up the troops from Meerut and Cawnpore; but for political reasons, already set forth, the Governor-General did not consider it advisable. The fact is, the Government of India did not think the Sikh army would ever actually cross the Sutlej. In January, 1845, they had prepared to move to the Sutlej, but the troops were withdrawn again, partly owing to the remonstrances of the political Agent; and the Government, presumably, expected much the same thing to occur again. The Governor-General was most anxious to avoid not only giving the Sikh

Government any pretext for alarm, but also taking any step which might not precipitate a war without ample cause for making it. Looking back on events that did occur, it cannot be doubted that he carried his prudence too far, and ran a much greater risk by neglecting the precaution of ordering up the Meerut troops. Nevertheless, he had greatly increased the strength of our forces on the frontier since his assumption of the Governor-Generalship. We were far more ready to meet a sudden emergency than we had been previous to his arrival; and all the available frontier troops, from Ferozepore to Umballa, were fully prepared for movement the moment the order should be given.

In these arrangements Sir Henry Hardinge and Sir Hugh acted together in perfect harmony.

On the 20th November Major Broadfoot wrote to Sir Hugh Gough, reporting that he had received Lahore letters, dated the the 18th, stating that the Durbar had ordered in writing the following plan of operations : Sikh army to be divided into seven divisions, of which one was to remain at Lahore, one to proceed to Peshawur, and five were to invade British India. Each division to be of from 8000 to 12,000 men. On this Sir Hugh Gough took on himself to order up some of the Meerut troops, and on the 25th a force of nearly 3000 men left Meerut for Umballa. He at the same time wrote to Sir Henry Hardinge, forwarding his order for confirmation or otherwise, as the Governor-General thought fit. The Governor-General was, as already stated, most averse to giving the Sikh Durbar any cause for apprehension; and as the next moment the aspect of affairs looked more peaceful, the order was countermanded, and the troops were ordered back to Meerut, where they arrived on the 30th November. This was unfortunate as had they been allowed to proceed they would have been up in time to join in the advance on Moodkee; but great pressure was put on the Governor-General by the Court of Directors to avoid all cause of offence, and not to interfere with the Punjab unless actual aggression was first perpetrated by the Sikhs; so that no further steps were taken to meet the coming storm. Meantime the Sikhs were endeavouring to tamper with the Hindostani sepoys, and many discharged sepoys, having been taken into the Sikh service, were employed in tempting our men to desert, using the high rate of pay as an incentive. A few instances occurred, but the fidelity of the native army stood the strain.

The plan of operations of the Sikh leaders on crossing the Sutlej seems to have been far from badly laid. Part of the force was to cut off Sir John Littler at Ferozepore, while, if possible, the Ludhiana force was to be met and crushed by the main body before the Umballa troops should have effected a junction; the theory being that the danger of Ferozepore would compel the Ludhiana force to advance at once in the hope of effecting a relief. The design, however, was frustrated, as will be seen, by the great marching achievement of the Umballa regiments.

At the beginning of December, the Governor-General, Sir Henry Hardinge, himself a very distinguished soldier, who had won the high approbation of the Duke of Wellington in the Peninsula, was near Ludhiana; the Commander-in-Chief being at Umballa. Sir Henry Hardinge's position was indeed a dangerously exposed one, considering the office he held, for his escort, consisting of only one regiment of native infantry besides his body-guard, could hardly have secured him from capture, had the Sikh cavalry possessed the enterprise to make the attempt. No such attempt was made, however, and accordingly he rode into Ludhiana in order to personally inspect the position and the fort. Seeing that this could be held by a small body, he desired Brigadier H.M. Wheeler to hold himself in readiness to march at the shortest notice, leaving the defence of the fort in the hands of the sick and weakly. On the 8th December he heard from Major Broadfoot, his political Agent, that there was no longer any doubt whatever that the Sikh were making preparations on large scale to cross the Sutlej and the following day he sent the too-long-deferred orders to the Commander-in-chief for the immediate advance of troops from Umballa, Meerut and elsewhere towards the frontier. On the 12th he heard of the actual crossing by the Sikhs, and on the 13th he issued his proclamation declaring war, dated from his camp about 25 miles from Ludhiana.

So complete had been the preparations for an advance that on the 12th the Commander-in-chief and the Umballa force marched 16 miles to Rajpura; on the 13th to Sirhind, 18 miles; on the 14th to Isru, 20 miles; on the 15th to Lattala, about 30 miles; and on the 16th to Wadni, 30 miles; overtaking the Governor-General, who with the Ludhiana troops had already marched to Bussean on their way to Ferozepore. Bussean was of great importance, as it was here that Major Broadfoot had stored the supplies which it had devolved upon him to collect (most successfully) by the most strenuous exertions at the shortest notice.

On the 17th the Governor-General and the Commander-in-chief marched with the now united columns of Ludhiana and Umballa to Charrak - a comparatively short stage – to give some rest to weary men and beasts; for the whole march up from Umballa had been exceptionally rapid, and through an exceedingly trying country. On the 18th they advanced 21 miles to Moodkee.

This march has been described in the diary of an officer, Captain Borton, of H.M.'s 9th Foot, afterwards General Sir Arthur Borton, as throughout most harassing; at one time over heavy ploughed land, then through low, thorny jungle, breaking all order, then again over

heavy sand. The dust surpassed all the writer's previous experience; the soldiers were sometimes the whole day without food, and when their meat rations were served out it often happened there were no means of cooking them, as the cooking-utensils had not come up. Yet, the troops marched bravely, though often straggling fearfully from fatigue and heat and dust.

On approaching Moodkee a patrol of the 9th Irregulars with Major Broadfoot reported it occupied by the Sikhs; and the British, formed in order of battle, marched in at noon, the small Sikh picquets retiring,

Thus about 150 miles had been covered by the troops in seven days over tracks heavy with sand, under clouds of dust which almost smothered the men in column, with little or no-water or regular food, and under a sun which was hot and oppressive in the day. This extra ordinarily rapid march of all available troops towards the frontier had been necessitated by the Sikh army, which for so long had been threatening an invasion, having at length crossed the Sutlej. Ferozepore, though held by a fairly strong garrison of about 7000 men, was more than 150 miles by the most direct route from the nearest support, and the sudden irruption of any army of 100,000 Sikhs with a powerful artillery was a source of danger which could not be ignored. It was perhaps also felt that forbearance had been carried already too far; that the Sikhs had been allowed to gain an advantage which nothing but very prompt and decisive measures could remedy. The Governor-General and the Commander-in-chief were most anxious to get near enough to Ferozepore to insure a combined movement with Littler's force and to relieve it from the pressure of the Sikhs. Within 24 hours of the receipt of orders the Umballa force was on the march, and Moodkee, about 20 miles from Ferozepore, was reached on the afternoon of the 18th.

The Engagement at Moodkee & After
December 18th – 21st

The country round Moodkee was a plain, with here and there slight risings, covered almost entirely with low, thorny jungle, the soil being heavy and sandy, so that the slightest movement of any body of men created an almost impenetrable dust.

Wearied with long and incessant marching, the troops were enjoying a well-earned rest when reports came in from the cavalry patrols that a large force of Sikhs, preceded by clouds of dust, was advancing upon them. Orders were at once issued to fall in, and in a very few minutes the force was formed in line of battle, the time being now about four o'clock in the afternoon.

The cavalry, together with the horse artillery, immediately advanced under Sir Hugh Gough's personal direction, and formed line in front of the Sikh position, the guns occupying the centre, flanked on the left by Brigadier Mactier, with the 9th Irregular Cavalry and a portion of the 4th Lancers, and on, the right by Brigadiers Gough and White, with the rest of the cavalry.

The infantry formed up in second line and moved forward; Wheeler's brigade, of H.M.'s 50th, the 42nd and 48th Native Infantry, on the extreme right, having Brigadier Bolton, with H.M.'s 31st and the 24th and 47th Native Infantry on their left, these regiments forming Sir Harry Smith's Division. Gilbert's Division, still incomplete, since the British regiments composing it had not yet joined, was only represented by one brigade of native troops: the 2nd and 16th Grenadiers and 45th Native Infantry.

These formed the centre, McCaskill's Division - H.M.'s 9th Foot, the 26th Native Infantry, the 73rd Native; Infantry, and H.M.'s 80th Foot, under Brigadier Wallace - being on the extreme left.

The field batteries having joined the Horse Artillery, a smart cannonade was opened. Then, in order to complete the infantry dispositions, the cavalry, first on the right and then also on the left, were ordered to make flank movements, turning the enemy's flank if possible, more especially because their line, extending beyond ours on either side, threatened to turn our left and right. Accordingly Brigadiers Gough and White, with the 3rd Light Dragoons, the Body-guard, the 3rd Light Cavalry, and a portion of the 4th Lancers, swept out to the right, and fell upon the enemy's left flank. The Sikh horse at once fled and the British and native cavalry swept down along the rear of the Sikh infantry, disconcerting the latter, and silencing their guns. While this manoeuvre was being brilliantly accomplished, Brigadier Mactier, sweeping to the left, fell upon the Sikh right in similar style, and with like success, completely everything all danger of the British line being outflanked. But for the jungle, the cavalry would have done even more complete execution.

Meantime the infantry, their front now uncovered, advanced upon the Sikh line in an echelon of brigades from the right, Sir Harry Smith's Division leading, and by their heavy fire soon convincing the Sikhs that they had met more than they expected; the artillery pushing on to close quarters, and maintaining an effective fire in support. The Sikh infantry and guns stood resolutely, fighting well and with great determination; but were steadily driven back by the British infantry, until they were forced to give way, and fled in great disorder. Darkness put an end to the pursuit, but the conflict was maintained in an irregular manner for another hour, clouds of dust still further obscuring every object.

Night saved the Sikh army from further disaster. Their loss was very severe, the ground being covered with their dead and wounded; and 17 guns were captured on the field. The troops did not get back to camp till midnight, fatigued and worn out by their arduous day's work and the severe fight: a sharp battle which foreshadowed the nature of the coming struggle with the Sikh army. Successful as it was, it was attended with very severe loss, particularly among the leaders and most distinguished officers of the army. Sir Robert Sale, Quartermaster-General of the British troops, was struck by a grape-shot which shattered his thigh, from the effects of which he died shortly afterwards. Sir John McCaskill was shot through the heart leading his division to the attack; and Brigadier Bolton, of H.M.'s 31st, received his death-wound at the head of the first brigade of Sir Harry Smith's Division; whilst Brigadiers Mactier and Wheeler were severely wounded, as also were Lieutenant-Colonel Byrne, commanding H.M.'s 31st Foot, and Major Pat Grant, Deputy-Adjutant-General of the army. The brunt of the fighting had fallen upon Sir Harry Smith's Division. The native infantry fought fairly well, but did not keep up with the European troops, and in the darkness that fell before the action was over some of our troops suffered from the fire of friends as well as foes.

The grand total of losses was :– Killed 13 officers, 2 native officers, 200 men = 215; Wounded 39 officers 9 native officers 600 men = 657; all ranks killed and wounded = 872.

Of the head-quarters' staff, 3 officers were killed and 3 wounded. The artillery lost 2 officers and 21 men killed, 4 officers, 1 native officer, and 42 men wounded, 45 horses killed and 25 wounded.

In the Cavalry Division, the 3rd Light Dragoons, who took 497 men into action, suffered most severely, losing 101 of all. ranks killed and wounded, and no less than 120 horses; the Native Cavalry lost 1 officer and 20 men killed, 6 officers, 1 native officer, and 43 men wounded. In Sir Harry Smith's Division the 31st Foot lost 175 all ranks killed and wounded; the 50th Regiment 125; the native corps, 1 officer 13 men killed; 7 officers 115 men wounded.

General Gilbert's Division lost 4 officers wounded, 1 native officer, 17 men killed; 5 native officers, 91 men wounded.

In Sir John McCaskill's Division, the only officer killed was its commander, and the loss generally was inconsiderable, but in proportion much heavier amongst the European than the native troops.

The returns published with despatches do not show the regimental losses, which have therefore been compiled from the regimental records.

In the despatches, the Sikh army was estimated at from 20,000 to 30,000 men, horse and foot, with 40 guns. It is most probable they advanced to attack the British under the supposition they would meet only the Ludhiana force, and that they were not aware that the Umballa force had already effected a junction. Other reports put the numbers as low as 2000 infantry, 10,000 horse, and 22 guns. The losses were never ascertained.

This was the first great combat with the Sikhs. Their gallantry and discipline in the fight evoked the admiration of their enemies, but their savage and barbarous treatment of the unfortunate wounded that happened to fall into their hands roused the most revengeful feelings on the part of British officers and men; for not only were the wounded horribly mutilated and slaughtered, but so treacherous and fanatical were they that even when their own lives had been spared by the order of officers, they were known in several instances to have fired on their deliverers, as soon as their backs were turned, and some fine gallant soldiers fell victims to their own generosity. So strong was the indignation excited in the 3rd Light Dragoons, who were horrified to find their comrades, who had fallen wounded in their splendid charge, cruelly murdered, that "Remember Moodkee," became a cry with them when they met the Sikhs again, and many were ruthlessly slain who would otherwise have been spared.

Mercy in the field of battle is not a thing understood by Orientals. One instance, however, deserves to be recorded to the credit of the Sikhs. About the time that the Sutlej was crossed, an officer, Lieutenant Biddulph, on his way to join his regiment at Ferozepore, fell into their hands, and although his life was in peril, it was spared, and he was made over to the charge of an officer of Sikh Artillery; the gunners became his friends; and, strange to say, after the Battle of Moodkee, he was allowed to return to the British camp, wither he was escorted by the artillery officer's brother. Sir Henry Hardinge very rightly would not allow Lieutenant Biddulph to take part in the subsequent battle at Ferozeshah; remarking that he owed that at least to the generous enemy who had released him. It is pleasant to be able to record occasional traits of civilisation and generosity on the part of our brave enemy, for, as a rule, their conduct on the field of battle was merciless in the extreme.

Another striking act of generosity will, however, fall to be related in connection with the Battle of Ferozeshah.

The following day the force halted in order to allow reinforcements to join, being now near enough in its position at Moodkee to render assistance to Littler's force in case of any urgent need. So that the principal object of the very rapid advance had been attained. In consequence, however, of the proximity of the Sikh army, the troops remained under arms all day, ready to fall in, in case the enemy should attempt a fresh attack.

The dead were as far as possible buried, and the wounded brought in; but owing to the very rapid advance at only a few hours' notice, the arrangements for the Field Hospital were by no means complete, and the sufferings of the wounded were great, without either proper shelter or food. The medical men worked, as they always do on such emergencies, with more than zeal, and did all that was possible; but rice-water and coarse wheaten cake, prepared for the elephants, were the only "hospital comforts" available.

Meantime such reinforcements as were at all within possible reach those, namely, from Kassauli and Subathu were hurrying up, eager to join the Commander-in-chief and take their share of the fighting they knew would have to take place before Ferozepore was relieved.

These reinforcements consisted of H.M.'s 29th Foot, and the 1st European Light Infantry, with a division of heavy guns and some native infantry.

The 29th Foot were quartered at Kassauli, and the 1st European Light Infantry at Subathu. Both regiments had received orders to be ready to move at a moment's notice. They received the orders for the march at very nearly the same time – that is, about 10 o'clock on the evening of the 10th December. The night was a busy one for all. A hurried medical examination was held at once, and all men unfit for active service, and those in hospital, were hurriedly told off to remain at regimental; headquarters, whilst the regiments were ordered to prepare for their march forthwith. Shortly before this compaign, Robert. Napier (subsequently Lord Napier of Magdala) saw the 1st European Light Infantry drawn up on parade at Subathu, numbering then nearly

1000 strong, and described its appearance as "glorious." About 60 men were left at Subathu; and by 10 o'clock on the morning of the 11th December, the regiment, probably about 800 strong, was in full march to join the Commander-in-Chief. In the same prompt manner the 69th Foot at Kassauli completed all its arrangements during the night of the 10th, and early on the morning of the 11th was on the march for Kalka, each man being served with 100 rounds of balled ammunition.

There was no "mobilization scheme" in those days, yet nothing could have been more prompt and effective than the rapid and highly disciplined manner in which all these troops moved off for the war. The 29th were one march nearer Kalka, at the foot of the hills, than the 1st European Light Infantry. The former regiment arrived there, received their camp equipage and transport without any delay from the commissariat department, and resumed their march in the afternoon for Munny Majra, doing twenty-three miles that day. Here they received orders to wait for the 1st European Light Infantry, who, likewise, on arriving at Kalka, were equipped for service, and reached Munny Majra on the 12th. On the 13th the two regiments, with the heavy guns, pushed on by double marches from 20 to 35 miles a day. On the 18th late in the evening, the sound of heavy firing in front announced that the war had begun in earnest. The troops struggled on to reach the field, but it was not possible, eager as they were; nor was it till the following evening, the 19th December, that they were able to join. They were sorely disappointed at not having been up in time for the first brush, but they had done all that could be done, and had covered nearly 200 miles in nine days' marching. Sir Henry Hardinge, always considerate for the soldiers, sent his own private elephants to help to bring the regiments in; a string of camels with fresh water was sent for the relief of the thirsty; whilst the bands of the regiments that had fought the battle of Moodkee the day before were sent out to march them in, so warmly were they welcomed, so fully were their efforts to join recognised by the Governor-General, the Commander-in-chief, and their comrades.

On the 20th, preparations were made to attack the enemy. No further reinforcements could possibly reach for weeks. The army could not remain in front of the Sikhs, waiting for them to come up. Ferozepore was partly invested, and open to an attack from the whole Sikh army; and it was necessary to relieve it and drive the Sikhs across the Sutlej. Accordingly sixty rounds of balled ammunition was served out to each man, and two days' cooked rations ordered to be carried with the troops, each man carrying all he could in his haversack, besides a bottle covered with leather slung over his shoulders for water. They were clothed in their ordinary scarlet uniform and blue trousers, and wore forage caps covered with white cloth, and a curtain hanging down behind for the protection of the head and neck; great coats were not carried.

There were no means of moving the large number of wounded, and consequently they were placed in a small fort at Moodkee. Two regiments of native infantry were all that could be spared for their protection, each regiment being ordered to detail one officer and a small party of men for their assistance.

Ferozepore was about 20 miles distant north-west from Moodkee, but the Sikh army, under Lall Singh, lay between the two. It might be possible to get Littler's force out by the south, and, effecting a junction with the Commander-in-chief, to make a combined attack upon Lall Singh. The British Force all told would then be about 18,000 men; but Littler had only one European Regiment, the 62nd

Foot, and it was quite possible that he might not be able to get away from Ferozepore without the knowledge of Tej Singh, who was lying before it; so that the junction could not be calculated on as a certainty. The Commander-in-chief, therefore, had to decide on his plan of operations in view of Littler not being able to join. He could not march round by the south and throw himself into Ferozepore, as that would have left the whole country open to the Sikh army, and his wounded at Moodkee, as to whose safety he was honourably solicitous, would have been at the cruel mercy of the Sikhs. Moreover, the armies of Lall Singh and Tej Singh, now known to be separated, would certainly have united and become more formidable then they were at present. Clearly, then, it would be advantageous to deal with Lall Singh whilst separate from Tej Singh, and to attack him - with the aid of Littler's force, if possible; if not, without. Accordingly secret and trustworthy messengers were sent to Sir John Littler, with orders for endeavouring to march out with as large a force as he could bring, consistently with the safety of Ferozepore, and without detection by the Sikhs; and so effecting a junction with the Commander-in-chief.

On this day also Sir Henry Hardinge, Governor-General of India, placed his services as a general officer at the disposal of the Commander-in-Chief. Whether right or wrong in his position, it was a noble and chivalrous act. He was a soldier of great experience and of the highest reputation, and had already, at Moodkee, shared the honour and the danger of battle with the army. His offer was accepted by Sir Hugh Gough with a full acknowledgment of its value, and he was appointed second in command.

Ferozepore was threatened on the north-east side by Rajah Tej Singh, with a force of all arms, immediately after the passage of the Sutlej. Sir John Littler told his force off into brigades; one cavalry brigade under Brigadier Harriott, consisting of the 8th Native Light Cavalry, and the 3rd Irregular Cavalry, each numbering about 300 men; the infantry in two brigades, of which H.M.'s 62nd, the 12th and 14th Regiments Native Infantry formed one under Brigadier Reid, of H.M.'s 62nd; while the other consisted of three native infantry regiments, the 33rd, 44th and 54th, under Brigadier, the Honourable T. Ashburnham, of the 62nd; and artillery, one European and one Native troop Horse Artillery, one field battery European, and one Native gunners, under Lieut.-Colonel Huthwaite, of the Artillery. The 63rd Regiment Native Infantry occupied the entrenchment, into which all the ladies, women, children, and sick of the station were sent; the 27th Native Infantry occupied and covered the city; while half a battery of artillery, and a squadron of irregular cavalry watched the ford at Koonda Ghat, to the north-west of the station.

A position was taken up by Sir John Littler to the north-east of cantonments, and he drew his small force up in order of battle on the 13th; Tej Singh, however, declined to make the attack, and Littler pitched his camp so as to cover the cantonments and the native city, the Sikh army having their camp within a short distance, and their outposts close up. The Sikhs made demonstrations threatening an attack on the 15th, 16th, and 17th; but though Littler drew out his force in the open, neither side precipitated a combat, for Littler, acting under particular instructions received from the Commander-in-Chief, would not be drawn away from his post, and whilst showing himself ready to engage, acted strictly on the defensive. On the evening of the 17th the approach of the Umballa force under the Commander-in-chief was reported, and was followed by intelligence of the battle of Moodkee and the repulse of the Sikh army. At midnight on the 20th Sir John Littler received his orders to move out the following morning in order to effect a junction with the Commander-in-chief. He arranged to move at 8 o'clock the following morning with the artillery, the cavalry brigade, and the two infantry brigades made up as described above, leaving the defence of the cantonments to the 63rd Regiment Native Infantry, under Lieut-Colonel Wilkinson, and that of the town to the 27th Native Infantry, with half a field battery in the town, and a battery of heavy guns in the cantonments, which was strengthened by entrenchments.

Ferozeshah: The Attack
December 21st

The force at Moodkee, under the immediate orders of Sir Hugh Gough, was called to arms in perfect silence at 2 a.m. on the 21st December; by 3 a.m. the camp had been struck and packed on camels, and by 4 a.m. the whole formed up in a line of coloumns preparatory to the march - four hours before Littler made his start from Ferozepore. Camp equipage and. all heavy baggage were left behind at Moodkee. In consequence of the arrival of the reinforcements, the previous distribution in brigades and divisions was modified. They now stood as, follows: –

Cavalry and *Artillery* the same as at Moodkee.

Infantry: First Division, under Major-General Sir Harry Smith; H.M.'s 31st Foot, the 24th and 47th Regiments Native Infantry, under Brigadier Hicks; the 2nd Brigade, H.M.'s 50th Foot, the 42nd and 48th Regiments Native Infantry, now commanded by Brigadier Ryan, of the 50th, vice Wheeler severely, wounded at Moodkee. Second Division, under Major-General Walter Raleigh Gilbert (a descendant of Sir Walter Raleigh, and worthy of his ancestor); H.M.'s 29th Foot, the 80th Foot, and the 41st Native Infantry, under Brigadier Taylor, of H.M.'s 29th; and the 1st European Light Infantry, with the 16th, Native Grenadiers and the 45th Native Infantry, under Brigadier McLaran.

Third Division, now commanded by Brigadier Wallace, vice Sir John McCaskill; consisting of H.M.'s 9th Foot, the 2nd Native Grenadiers, the 26th and 73rd Regiments Native Infantry.

The army advanced for about four miles in a line of columns, ready to deploy into line in case the Sikhs should be met with; but when it was ascertained that the enemy had concentrated about his entrenched position at Ferozeshah, they moved in a column of route, left in front.

The advance was necessarily slow, owing to the broad front of the army, the darkness, and the rough nature of the country; the road being a mere track through the jungle. At about half-past ten the Sikh position was approached; and the troops halted, and were allowed to rest a while and get a scratch breakfast from their haversacks, whilst the Commander-in-chief rode forward to make a personal reconnaissance. Littler's force had not yet joined, but it was ascertained that he was on his way, and his junction was secure.

The Sikh army was in two divisions. One under Tej Singh lay on the north of Ferozepore, facing Sir John Littler's contonments. The second, and larger, under Lall Singh, had occupied a position at the village of Frozeshah, between Moodkee and Ferozepore, some two miles on the northern side of the line of march. Here they had formed batteries, and thrown up entrenchments (within which was the village), shaped roughly like a horseshoe. The toe, or central front, faced towards the south, and lay more or less parallel to the British line of march. The right wing faced westward, in the direction of Ferozepore; and the left eastward, in the direction of Ludhiana. Thus, Sir John Littler, starting from Ferozepore, would march out in a southeasterly direction, leaving Tej Singh on the north and east of his cantonments. The force under the Commander-in-chief, arriving from Moodkee, might either give battle to Lall Singh or march on towards Ferozepore; but this, of course, would leave the whole country eastwards, including Moodkee, open to the advance of Lall Singh.

While the troops were breakfasting, the Commander-in-Chief rode forward to make a personal reconnaissance, as the result of which he formed the following plan of action. Knowing definitely that Littler's force was on the way, and was secure of effecting the junction, he resolved to leave it the duty of acting as a reserve, and to himself at once attack the position at Ferozeshah with the whole of his three divisions, without waiting for Sir John. The arguments in favour of this plan of action were strong. By making the attack early in the day the troops would be able to do their work while fairly fresh; and in Sir Hugh's judgment, supported by the event, they might then be relied on to carry the entrenchments and drive the Sikhs back Meantime, if Tej Singh advanced from Ferozepore, Littler would hold him in check, or if he did not advance would be able to fall on Lall Singh's engaged army and effect a complete rout. On the other hand, delay would mean that the day might close before the engagement was decisively at an end, and would be accompanied by the risk of Tej Singh's arrival at a critical time.

The Commander-in-chief explained his plan of action to the Governor-General, who was also second in command in the field; but Sir Henry was flatly and resolutely opposed to it. In his view, the issue at stake was so serious, and the Sikhs had already at Moodkee shown such high fighting qualities, that he considered it imperative to wait till the junction with Littler was accomplished before proceeding to the attack.

Now, Sir Henry Hardinge, as things stood, occupied a very anomalous position. As Governor-General, he was responsible for the safety of the British dominion in India, but as a matter of course a civilian Governor-General cannot be held responsible for military operations. On the other hand, previous military Governors-General had combined that office with the-Commander-in-Chiefship. There was no precedent for his position. An experienced military officer, he had a very strong opinion as to the military necessaries of the position which was in flat contradiction to that of his Commander-in-chief, whose view was equally strong. Sir High Gough could not surrender his judgment in favour of that of his subordinate in the field; Sir Henry could not escape his own sense of responsibility. Taking this view, there was only one course open - as Governor-General, he must overrule the Commander-in-Chief on the very field of battle, and in the presence of the enemy.

The affairs must have been painful enough for both; but it is clear that the responsibility for the serious results which followed this historic incident falls entirely upon Sir Henry Hardinge. The Commander-in-Chief had no option in the matter; Sir Henry could and did simply overrule him. But, to his honour, it can be said that no man ever more resolutely and loyally carried out the Governor-General's wishes than did Sir Hugh Gough; and from this moment, throughout the critical events which immediately followed, no trace or hint appears of the vexation which he might legitimately have felt.

When, after considerable discussion, this decision had bee arrived at, the troops were ordered to move to their left, and at about one o'clock the junction with Littler was effected, at the village of Shukur, close to Misreewalla, some 3000 yards south-west of the enemy's extended position. Sir John had accomplished his withdrawal from Ferozepore with great skill, and entire success. Leaving his camp standing, and his picquets out as usual, he had thoroughly deceived Tej Singh, and had marched out on the southern side at about eight o'clock in the morning, without arousing a suspicion in the mind of the Sikhs -

who remained watching the empty shell while the army went on its way to join the forces from Moodkee.

By waiting for the actual junction, valuable time had been lost; for it must be remembered that the day was December 21st, the shortest in the year. The arrival of the fresh column, moving in another direction, involved further delay before the troops could be got into position; and it was close upon four o'clock before the attack commenced. By this time, the force that marched from Moodkee had been already nearly fourteen hours under arms; that from Ferozepore nearly eight hours under a hot sun, and marching over a heavy sandy country in clouds of dust, with scarcely a drop of water.

The army then was drawn up fronting the southern and western faces of the Sikh position, with Littler's division on the left, Wallace's in the centre, and Gilbert's on the right, Sir Harry Smith's forming in reserve. A powerful battery, including the heavy guns, was placed between the divisions of Gilbert and Wallace, and batteries of horse artillery on the flanks. White's Cavalry Brigade, 3rd Light Dragoons and 4th Bengal Lancers, protected the right, whilst Gough's Brigade, consisting of the Governor-General's Bodyguard and 5th Cavalry, was in support of Wallace; and Harriott's Brigade, 8th Light Cavalry and 3rd Irregulars, supported Littler's Division, he having also with him the artillery from Ferozepore.

By four o'clock the action had commenced, and the first gun was fired. The British artillery came into action within effective range all along the front, and poured their fire on the Sikh position, our infantry being ordered to lie down. The enemy's artillery, however, responded vigorously, and, after heavy pounding on both sides, it became apparent that our guns were quite unable to gain the mastery of the Sikhs, who had a considerable superiority both in number of guns and weight of metal; while the day was drawing to a close. Our artillery therefore advanced to closer quarters, supported by the infantry.

Littler's division somewhat prematurely advanced to the attack, on the Sikh right or westerly front, under a most galling fire; and, to quote his description, "the casualties were awful." Brigadier Reid led the right brigade, the 62nd Foot and 12th Native Infantry in first line, the 14th Native Infantry in support. The advance was conducted with perfect steadiness, notwithstanding that the nature of the country made occasional breaks in the line. As they approached the entrenchments the ground became more open and the enemy's fire increased to a storm of grape. The line approached the enemy's battery to within about one hundred and fifty yards, when the prize seemed to be within their grasp; but it chanced to be the strongest part of the position, defended by numerous guns of heavy calibre, although the entrenchments were no stronger than elsewhere. The native infantry regiments had to a certain extent, melted away, and the 62nd was assailed by a terrific fire. Sir John Littler, Brigadier Reid, and all the officers cheered and encouraged the men; but, unable to advance, the 62nd were brought to a stand. So fierce was the firing that, within a few minutes, 7 officers and 97 men were killed, and 11 officers and 184 men wounded. Lieutenants Gubbins and Kelly fell from sabre cuts, close to the entrenchments, and many individuals distinguished themselves in setting a brilliant example of courage. But the regiment was almost alone and unsupported; the Sikh cavalry were threatening their left; and Brigadier Reid at length, to save the regiment from further useless destruction, ordered them to retire, seeing the hopelessness of carrying the enemy's works.

This movement was executed in good order and with deliberation,

the men, in fact, being so exhausted as to be scarcely able to put one foot before the other, till they came upon H.M.'s 9th Foot and the 26th Native Infantry who were formed in reserve. The Divisional Staff lost 1 officer killed and 1 wounded, and Brigadier Reid and 1 officer of the Brigade Staff were wounded. The 12th Native Infantry, which advanced with the 62nd, lost 4 officers wounded, and the 14th Native Infantry 5. The other losses of the native infantry-regiments amounted to 3 native officers and 47 men killed, 5 native officers and 164 men wounded. As far as can be ascertained from the returns of casualties, the second brigade, on the extreme left, commanded by Brigadier Ashburnbam, and consisting of three native infantry regiments, suffered no loss whatever, and cannot have afforded any support to Brigadier Reid. The Sikhs paid all their attention to the European troops; and Ferozeshah was unfortunately not one of the sepoy's "fighting days." As a matter of fact, the Hindostani sepoys of those times had not the stamina to stand the long and hard day's work, and were far more exhausted than the European troops.

The news of Littler's repulse went down the line before the attack of the centre and right was made. It was announced by wild shouts of triumph among the Sikhs, whose hopes of victory were greatly raised by it, but it in no way affected the Moodkee force, unless perhaps it made them even more determined to succeed. The assault was ordered in direct echelon from the right, Brigadier Taylor leading with H.M.'s 29th in advance, closely and vigorously supported by H.M.'s 80th, and after them the 41 st Regiment Native Infantry; under the direct personal leading of the Commander-in-chief, who took the right of the line, whilst Sir Henry Hardinge took command of the centre. Covered by a line of skirmishers, the 29th advanced in quick time with the utmost steadiness, not withstanding the heavy fire it was exposed to, which swept away sometimes whole sections; Brigadier Taylor, himself being grazed by a round shot in the side, was removed from the field, suffering much from the shock. The 80th, eager to bear their full share of the honour and danger of the fight, pressed on so close as almost to form in prolongation of the 29th. The two regiments cheered each other as they advanced. Unflinchingly, and pouring in a heavy fire, Taylor's brigade charged up the entrenchments, but only to find on crossing them that though they had got the guns, the Sikh infantry stood unsubdued behind them. The men, however, pushed gallantly and resolutely on, driving the enemy back at the point of the bayonet, and entered the Sikh camp. Here the 80th came upon a number of the enemy clad in chain armour, who suddenly rushed upon the regiment and inflicted considerable loss before they were bayoneted.

Brigadier Taylor's attack was rapidly followed by Brigadier McLaran with the 1st Bengal European Light Infantry, and the 16th and 45th Regiments Native Infantry. Major Birrell commanding the 1st, wisely ordered the regiment to reserve their fire until they came to close quarters with the enemy. As the line advanced the fire from the Sikh guns increased in intensity, the round shot and shell tearing through the ranks. Many officers and men fell; but the brigade, led by the 1st Europeans, continued its steady advance. As they approached close to the enemy's battery, the order was given to charge, and in a few minutes the regiment was right under the batteries, the smoke being so dense that it was almost as dark as night. The Sikhs had thrown down branches of trees to form a sort of entanglement. Surmounting these, the men were soon amongst the guns. The Sikh gunners, fighting desperately, were bayoneted to a man; behind them the Khalsa Infantry was drawn up, and their camp stood visible in rear. The infantry, dropping on one knee as if to receive cavalry, opened a galling fire; but with a cheer McLaran's Brigade, the 1st leading, charged. The Sikhs fired a wild volley and broke; many drew their swords and fought to the death, compact bodies again and again dashing at the colours. At length, however, they gave way, seeking cover amidst their tents; though hard work still remained, as will presently be told.

Thus Gilbert's Division had been completely successful in its assault, which was followed almost immediately by a magnificent charge by the glorious 3rd Light Dragoons, Led by White, and accompanied by a troop of Horse Artillery, they had followed up the attack of the right. Now, advancing through a most destructive fire of grape and musketry, their leaders falling in numbers, they charged undismayed over the Sikh entrenchments with loud huzzas, dashed through the Sikh infantry, silenced their guns, cut down the gunners, swept right through the enemy's camp, and finally emerged among their friends with numbers thinned, but, as it was said at the time, "covered with imperishable glory."

Wallace's Division next followed, and was directed partly against the portion of the enemy's position from which Littler's Division had been already repulsed, i.e. the left central face, The four regiments of which the division was composed were being temporarily formed in two brigades - that on the left consisting of the 9th Foot and 26th Native Infantry, led by Colonel Taylor of the 9th; the 2nd and 73rd Regiments Native Infantry being on the right.

The smoke and dust combined were so thick that it was impossible to see the exact position' of the enemy's guns; the left wing of the 9th found itself immediately in front of the muzzles, and suffered terribly, Colonel Taylor and many officers and men being killed. So severe was the fire that a portion of the regiment was for a time thrown into confusion; but, although himself very severely wounded by a grape shot in the right arm, Captain Borton, the senior officer on the spot, rallied them; and the right pressing on with great dash the guns were captured at the point of the bayonet. Here, in the increasing darkness, the Grenadier company under Lieutenant Daunt, with part of the right wing of the 9th under Major Burnewell, got separated from the remainder of the regiment, and falling in with a party separated from McLaran's Brigade, which formed the left of Gilbert's Division in their movement to their left, advanced with them upon the village of Ferozeshah; which was found to have been captured by Sir Harry Smith, who, having been placed in reserve, had been ordered by the Commander-in-chief to follow up Gilbert's attack, in view of the severe fighting on the right. With this force that portion of the 9th remained till next day.

Sir Harry Smith had formed in rear of the centre of the line, his right brigade led by Brigadier Hicks, and his left by Brigadier Ryan. As they advanced they came under a heavy fire, and passing through a gap in the first line, charged the entrenchments, cheered on by Sir Harry, who shouted, 'Into them, my lads; the day is your own!" Here fell Major Broadfoot, the Governor-General's political Agent, shot through the heart, having already been once knocked off his horse by another shot - a brave and invaluable officer, whose thorough knowledge of frontier affairs was most useful to the Governor-General. Smith pressed with Ryan's (the left) Brigade into the Sikh camp, driving all before him, and then coming upon the village of Ferozeshah, stormed and captured it; but in the confusion and darkness which was fast falling, his right brigade, under Brigadier Hicks, was separated from him, adhering to Gilbert's Division.

After carrying the entrenchment, as narrated, Gilbert's Division had been involved in a further struggle. His left brigade (McLaran's), with the 1st European Light Infantry leading, had wheeled to their left, and were charging along the line of the Sikh entrenchments, capturing and spiking many guns, when orders were received to secure the village of Ferozeshah. Towards this they now bent their way, but before they had gone more than 200 yards the men were suddenly scattered by the explosion of a large magazine of powder, the air being filled with smoke and fire, which, as it cleared away, exposed to view a number of gallant soldiers lying frightfully mutilated. This fearful explosion in the rapidly approaching darkness scattered the regiment so much that scarcely 150 men remained with the colours of the 1st Europeans, whilst the fire spread, causing other and. smaller explosions, all adding to the confusion McLaran's Brigade, however, now greatly reduced in numbers, continued its advance on the village; but finding it already in possession of Sir Harry Smith, returned towards the line of the entrenchments.

A number of men of the 1st Europeans, scattered by the explosions, were collected by their officers, and falling in, as related, with a portion of the 9th Foot, joined Sir Harry Smith in the village of Ferozeshah. Parched with thirst, the men, seeing some wells near by, sought for water, when the Sikhs from the camp suddenly opened fire on them.

Lieutenant Greville of the 1st, the senior officer on the spot, led his men against the Sikhs, but was met by so severe a fire from a barricade the enemy had built up that they were forced back. Lieutenant Moxon, carry one of the colours, was killed immediately in front of the barricade, when Lieutenant Percy Innes, seeing the colour lying on the ground, rushed back alone and brought it off amidst the cheers of the men. Lieutenant Greville, leading a second charge, succeeded in driving off the Sikhs and capturing the barricade. Darkness was now rapidly increasing, and with it confusion.

The Sikh camp was on fire, and frequent explosions

were taking place; there became a danger of the troops firing into each other. The Commander-in-chief therefore wisely decided to withdraw the scattered troops from the Sikhs camp, and to form a bivouac in the open space about 300 yards from the entrenchments.

The assembly, with the various regimental calls, was sounded. At length, after much search, the regiments, which had got considerably mixed were collected and formed up.

It will indeed be obvious that the confusion was very great. Sir Harry Smith, with Brigadier Ryan's Brigade and detachments of various regiments, principally the 9th and 1st European Light Infantry from Taylor's and McLaran's Brigades respectively, with scattered bodies of sepoys, remained in the village, but without knowing the position occupied by any other troops. Owing to the sudden arrival of the darkness, the day being the shortest of the year, they were enveloped in its shades before Sir Harry Smith had means of ascertaining the whereabouts of the rest of the force, or of communicating his own position to the Commander-in-chief. He formed up the 50th in a square on the eastern side of the village, the detachment of the other corps forming another square, irregular, but effective. These retained their position all through the night, although harassed by the enemy's fire and by parties of Sikhs prowling round in the darkness.

Littler's repulsed brigades had drawn up westwards, near Misreewalla, but this was not known to the other divisions.

In this position the British troops, with the Commander-in-Chief and the Governor-General of India in their midst, passed the night of the 21st December. The attack had been on the point of success when night put an end to the conflict. It is impossible to say exactly what was the position of the troops, but it was certain that the losses had been very severe. Littler's Division had been repulsed, and its position was unknown, while Sir Harry Smith, with a portion of his brigade, was missing. The men and officers were all worn out with fatigue, having been at work since 2 a.m.; hungry and without food, parched with thirst and without a drop of water, bitterly cold, without great-coats or any shelter, and unable to light fires without bringing down the fire of the enemy; and all this after a terribly severe struggle, while the Sikhs still maintained an incessant fire, and made the darkness more hideous with their shouts and clamour.

That night, when, as it has well been said, "the fate of India trembled in the balance," was a truly awful one for all; most so for the Commander-in-chief and the Governor-General, while it tried the nerve of the most resolute and intrepid.

The Commander-in-chief did not, indeed, disguise from himself the critical nature of affairs; but he never for one moment wavered. Sternly and firmly he remained fixed to his decision to fight it out in the morning, fully relying on the discipline, courage, and tenacity of his British regiments. There were, indeed, those who would have counselled retreat; to one such he replied, "Better that our bones should bleach honourably on the field of battle, than retire." Sir Henry Hardinge was equally resolved, and entirely supported the chief; and their courageous determination proved the highest wisdom. No troops in the world could have behaved better than the Englishmen. Fatigue, hunger, thirst, the bitter cold, the losses they had suffered, the groans of their wounded comrades, the yells and incessant firing of the enemy - all theses failed to shake their nerve. Animated and encouraged by the noble example of their commanders, and placing full reliance on their leading, they faced the worst with stern resolve to drive the enemy out in the morning. But even brave and experienced officers were forced afterwards to admit that they had the most gloomy anticipations; knowing that the attack was to be renewed in the morning, they had uneasy doubts as to the result, for the native troops were much disheartened and unnerved by the carnage of the two preceding fights. The stern valour of the English troops and their indomitable courage was felt to be the sole and only resource.

Up to this time a gallant and distinguished officer, Prince Waldemar of Prussia, a member of the royal family, had accompanied the Governor-General through all this severe fighting, attended by some of his own friends, one of whom had already met a soldier's death upon the field. But now Sir Henry Hardinge felt it would not be right to allow him to risk his valuable life in a cause not his own, and to his great disappointment and vexation, Sir Henry insisted upon Prince-Waldemar leaving the field and proceeding to Ferozepore. The prince was filled with regret at not being allowed to remain with the comrades he had learnt to love and respect, and to share their dangers to the end. He was, however, allowed subsequently to rejoin, and came in for further fighting at Sobraon.

The Sikhs had also suffered terrible losses, had been driven from their entrenchments, and, though much shattered and to a considerable extent demoralised by the combat, still clung to the interior of the position. But when they found that the British force had evacuated the entrenchments, they reoccupied them and opened fire upon the British bivouac. One gun causing especial annoyance, Sir Henry Hardinge at length called on H.M.'s 80th, with the 1st Europeans, to "Silence that gun." They responded gallantly, Colonel Bunbury, leading with the 80th, assisted by Lieut.-Colonel Wood, an aide-de-camp to the Governor-General, and supported by the 1st, under Major Birrell. In perfect silence they advanced straight upon the gun till within a short distance, when they charged, bayoneting the gunners, spiking the gun, and completely dispersing the enemy. This gallant and very decisive episode showed the Sikhs beyond any doubt that they had not yet done with the English army, and gave a comparative peace to the weary troops for the remainder of the night.

Whilst this, the main portion of the army, consisting of the. divisions of Gilbert and Wallace, and part of Smith's, together with the artillery and most of the cavalry, were lying outside to the south of the Sikh entrenchments, Sir Harry Smith, with his one brigade, held on to the village of Ferozeshah, in the centre of the Sikh position. To them also it was a terribly trying night, nor could they ascertain what had become of the rest of the army, nor whether they were conquerors or conquered. In this state of isolation, and without any apparent support, Sir Harry Smith decided to evacuate the village before daylight and to rejoin the rest of the army as best he could. Accordingly, at 3 a.m. he withdrew his troops by the south-west, corner, and, guided by the lights of a bivouac, effected a junction with Sir John Littler, who after his repulse had drawn up his force in the neighbourhood of Misreewalla.

Ferozashah: Second Day
December 22nd

So closed the memorable night of the 21st December; though not, for some hours yet, the Battle of Ferozeshah.

At the first appearance of the dawn, that portion of the army under the immediate orders of the Commander-in-chief, formed line to renew the attack. Sir Hugh Gough placed himself at the head of the right, and Sir Henry Hardinge at the left of the line; Gilbert and Wallace at the head of their respective divisions. H.M.'s 31st, with the remains of the native corps attached to it, were on the extreme right. The Horse Artillery occupied the flanks, the heavy guns and a rocket battery the centre. These opened as effective a fire as they could pour in upon the Sikhs; under cover. of which the infantry advanced in magnificent style unchecked by the enemy's fire, till the charge was sounded. Thereupon the whole line rushed upon the Sikhs, driving them in headlong flight at the point of the bayonet; then changed front to their left, swept the camp, and dislodged the enemy from their whole position. The line then halted, and drew up victorious on that well-fought battlefield, receiving both Sir Hugh Gough and Sir Henry Hardinge with loud and prolonged cheers, as they rode together down the line. The division of Sir John Littler, with Sir Harry-Smith's 2nd brigade, now rejoining, the whole army was concentrated in the Sikh position.

The troops which had been over twenty-four hours under the severest physical and nervous strain, with scarcely any food, and but little water, were fairly exhausted; but at last it seemed as if their labour was over, and they might get water and refreshments from the village and the camp. They were in the highest spirits, and already congratulating each other over their hardwon victory, when intelligence was sent back by the cavalry following up the retreat, to the north, of the defeated Sikhs that a fresh Sikh force was approaching from the direction of Ferozepore. The approach of these newcomers was presently heralded by huge clouds of dust. Tej Singh had spent the whole of the previous day watching, as he thought, Littler's force.

Hearing the heavy fire in the evening, and probably finding that Littler had moved out, he had marched in the early morning of the 22nd to the assistance of Lall Singh; and now arrived upon the scene with some 30,000 cavalry and infantry and a large field of artillery. It is impossible to say whether he expected to find Lall Singh still in possession of his entrenched position; but it must soon have been made clear to him that the British were now entire masters of the field, and that the Sikhs had fled.

Our position, however, was now most critical. There was a perfectly fresh army to face; our men had had no opportunity for rest or refreshment; the ammunition was all but exhausted; the cavalry horses were so worn out by the long-continued work and want of food that many of them could hardly raise a trot. On the other hand, the Sikhs, brave and stubborn as they showed themselves in defence, never displayed equal capacity in the attack, owing, no doubt, in part, to want of training and ability in their leaders. Moreover, they were ignorant of the straits in which we were; whilst they plainly realised that our army had driven Lall Singh from his entrenchments and were now clearly determined to hold them.

Tej Singh drew up his army, sending his artillery to the

front and opening a heavy fire which was maintained with great vigour. An energetic attempt was made to turn our left flank, which was repulsed; this was followed by a similar attack and repulse on the right; and then the Sikhs began to fall back. It has been believed by many that Tej Singh took alarm at a movement on the part of the bulk of our cavalry and horse artillery, which had been ordered by an officer of the head-quarters staff to proceed to Ferozepore. That order has never been explained – it was wholly unauthorised; and the officer who gave it (who is said to have been suffering from sunstroke) was subsequently removed from his appointment, and severely reprimanded. But Tej Singh, unable to account for this curious movement, appears to have jumped to the conclusion that it was intended to attack him in the rear. At any rate, he began to fall back, when a bold dash of a squadron of the 3rd Light Dragoons, supported by a portion of the 4th Bengal Lancers, into the middle of the horde of Sikh cavalry, them flying. This charge was led by Brigadier White in person, and as they galloped past Gilbert's Division in their attack, that fine old soldier rode up and joined in the charge.

The second Sikh attack, and the fire of their heavy artillery, had been a great strain on the endurance, discipline, and pluck of our troops, and occasioned considerable loss; amongst others, Brigadier Wallace of H.M.'s 9th Foot, commanding the 3rd Division, was killed by a round shot.

During this cannonade, Sir Hugh Gough was so deeply moved at seeing his brave infantry, soldiers who had fought so nobly, subjected to the severe fire, that he rode out to the flank of the force, accompanied by one aide-de-camp, and placed himself in a conspicuous position, in order to draw the fire of the Sikh guns away from his men. The shot struck all round him, but neither Sir Hugh nor his gallant steed moved, nor were even touched, though His Excellency had had one horse struck by a round shot in the earlier part of the battle.

Tej Singh had now become aware of the tremendous carnage which had taken place in the course of expelling Lall Singh's troops from their entrenchments. From this knowledge he appears to have derived a conviction that it would be utterly useless to attempt dislodging from those entrenchments the men who had carried them with such manifest valour in the face of a resistance so conspicuously stubborn. Accordingly, he now withdrew, suddenly and entirely, and commenced a hasty retreat northward and towards the Sutlej. Detractors have affirmed that he merely wished for a plausible pretext; but the defence given is the one he himself subsequently alleged for his action; nor does it appear unreasonable. He did not know how exhausted our men were, nor that ammunition was failing; he did know that the troops before him were behind entrenchments out of which they had thrashed the flower of the Sikh , while his own troops were chiefly irregulars. Had he been inspired with the enthusiasm of the Khalsa, he might have acted differently; but there is no real ground for questioning the honesty of his explanation.

Whatever Taj Singh's motive was, the sight of his army in hurried retreat was singularly welcome to the British troops. "They had now been under arms for upwards of forty hours; they had had neither food nor water since the previous morning; they had been ceaselessly exposed to the most fatiguing work; the additional strain of anxiety, during the past night especially, had been intense; and for a great part of the time they had been engaged in actual hard fighting with a powerful and most stubborn foe. Now at last the weary troops, completely tired out and exhausted by their two days' sanguinary contest, and the want of food and water, could seek shelter and refreshment. Fortunately the Sikh camp and village of Ferozeshah afforded both, large stores of grain having been collected by the enemy; besides which several bullock were found and promptly killed.

The wounded, many of whom had been lying for twenty-four hours on the ground untended, were now looked after. Their sufferings had been terrible, and many had fallen victims to the merciless cruelty of the Sikhs; but it is again gratifying to be able to give one instance of humanity on the part of the enemy. Lieutenant Sievwright, an officer of H.M.'s 9th Foot, had been desperately wounded in front of the Sikh battery, and lay all that; night in dreadful anguish on the field with a shattered leg, helpless and unable to move. At daylight, finding that the Sikhs were cutting up the unprotected wounded, he managed with incredible difficulty to drag himself some short way further off. Seeing a Sikh soldier approaching, Sievwright grasped his pistol and challenged him; to his relief, the Sikh replied, "Salaam, sahib." Seeing that he was clearly kindly disposed, Sievwright called him up; the man sat down beside him, and after some conversation it was arranged that the Sikh soldier should carry him to the nearest succour. This good Samaritan took his wounded foe on his back, and carried him, at the peril of his own life, some-two miles to the rear, where he met a dooli, in which Sievwright was placed, and conveyed into Ferozepore. Acts of kindness between enemies have often been heard of on a battle-field, but never one that could surpass this. The Sikh remained with Lieutenant Sievwright, and tended him in hospital; but it is melancholy to relate that the gallant young officer himself died only a week after from the effects of his wound, which necessitated the amputation of his leg above the knee. Records do not show what became of the brave and kind-hearted Sikh, but it may be certain that his generous humanity did not pass unrewarded.

The list of casualties in this great battle shows not only how stubborn was the fighting, but also how entirely the brunt of it was borne by the European troops. Sir Hugh

Gough himself had one horse killed under him, and one of his personal staff, Lieutenant - now Field-Marshal Sir Frederick Haines severely wounded. The Governor-General had every member of his staff disabled, and Major Broadfoot was killed. Brigadier Wallace, in command of a division, was killed. General Gilbert, commanding a division, had one horse killed and another wounded under him; and Brigadiers Harriott, White and Taylor, were all wounded.

It is difficult to ascertain the actual strength of regiments in action. The European infantry regiments probably numbered about 5600, making up about 6000 with the grand old 3rd Light Dragoons, who had already lost nearly 100 killed and wounded at Moodkee, and cannot now have amounted to more than 400 men. On the other hand, the 15 regiments native infantry, and 5 regiments native cavalry, must have made up 10,000; but the losses were : –

Killed : officers, British, 37, native, 17; men, British, 462, native, 178; total, 694.

Wounded : officers, British, 78, native, 18; men, British, 1054, native, 571; total, 1721.

Grand total of all ranks killed and wounded, 2415.

The losses of the British regiments are given in detail in a footnote. Proud indeed may those regiments be of the part they played in the battle of Ferozeshah.

Seventy-three guns had been captured on the field; a Sikh army of over 60,000 men had been completely routed, and the enemy driven over the frontier. The Duke of Wellington, writing to Sir Hugh Gough, on receipt of his news of Ferozeshah, lamented the heavy losses, but added these words: "Long experience has taught me that such achievements cannot be performed, and such objects attained as in these operations without great loss, and that in point of fact the honour acquired by all is proportionate to the difficulties and dangers met and overcome."

Before leaving Ferozeshah, it is necessary once more to revert to the conflict of opinion between the Governor-General and the Commander-in-chief. No one will dispute that Sir Henry Hardinge acted in a manner which must have been most distasteful to him, and under stress of a strong sense of duty, an entire conviction that the Commander-in-chief's plan involved a risk which it was out of the question for him to sanction. For the plan which was followed, Sir Henry took the responsibility which was his and his only, although some of those who blamed the course taken have spoken as if Sir Hugh Gough was to be held accountable. Opinions may differ as to the wisdom of the course chosen; there is no room whatever for difference as to the responsibility for choosing it. On the other hand, the consequences of that choice are perfectly clear. The attack was delayed so long that night came on before the Sikhs were fairly driven from their position, the British brigades lost each other in the darkness, heavy losses were incurred, and a fresh fight with fresh troops had to be carried on through the greater part of the following day without time or opportunity for food or refreshment. It may indeed be argued that no one can tell what would have happened had the Commander-in-chief been allowed to carry out his plan. Looking at the facts, however, it seems difficult to doubt that plan would have met with complete success. It was opposed broadly on the ground that the Sikh position could not be carried without Sir John Littler's force; but when that force joined, one half of it, Ashburnham's Brigade, never seems to have come fairly into action, and the other half was repulsed. The approach of night greatly increased the hurry and consequent confusion; yet before the darkness fell, the Moodkee force, and the Moodkee force alone, had carried the entrenchment, and would, it may be said with certainty, have driven the Sikhs completely out of their position - as they did the next morning - with another two hours of daylight to do it in. Had this same force made the attack at twelve o'clock instead of at four, while still comparatively fresh, the Sikhs must have been completely routed. Littler's force would have arrived early in the engagement, in time to give whatever support was required; whereas in the actual battle, from the time of its repulse, which preceded the advance of the right and centre, it rendered no assistance whatever. The plan of the Commander-in-chief, in fact, bears a remarkable resemblance to that of Moltke at Koniggratz, when, instead of waiting for a junction to be completed, he attacked the Austrians; the second army coming up and attacking the enemy in flank during the engagement - thus achieving a decisive victory.

Even if the attack had met with an initial check, Sir John would have been in time to prevent disaster. The horror of the night of December 21st would have been escaped; the British troops would have had that food and water which were so sorely needed, and would have faced Tej Singh the next day recuperated instead of exhausted.

Still it must be remembered that with the smaller force the possibility of a complete repulse would have been greater, and its effects terrific. Sir Henry accounted that risk too tremendous to be incurred; very much as in 1857 General Wilson, before Delhi, could hardly be persuaded to sanction the storming, in which failure would have meant the loss of India.

Sir Henry's action may be deplored or applauded, and Sir Hugh's generalship commended or condemned, according to the judgment of the critic; but whatever view may be taken of the Governor-General's interference, his personal conduct in the presence of the crisis, the splendid example he showed of courage, of resolution, of calmness, or, in one word, of grit,. are beyond all praise; and their effect on the spirit of the men on that night when "the fate of India trembled in the balance" can never be over-estimated.

Budhowal And Aliwal:
December 23th – January 28th

The Sikh army, shattered, and having lost nearly 100 guns and about 5000 men, retired from Ferozeshah and recrossed the Sutlej, just ten days after the invasion whilst the Commander-in-Chief encamped at Sultan Khan Walla, watching the frontier and awaiting the arrival of the troops which had been ordered to advance from the more distant stations of Meerut, Delhi and Cawnpore, at the same time as those from Umballa and the hill stations. On the 27th December, Sir Hugh Gough advanced to Arufkee, and personally pushed a reconnaissance to the fords at Sobraon, where the enemy were to be seen encamped on the right bank of the river. Sir Harry Smith's Division was placed at Malowal, from which point he maintained a careful watch on the enemy.

In the meantime the Sikhs had not been idle. Short as the time was, they had already brought up a fresh supply of guns from Lahore and were almost as well furnished with artillery as before, whilst their army was rehabilitated and reinforced by large bodies of well-trained soldiers. By the 5th January they were showing renewed signs of aggression and making predatory incursions across the Sutlej, in the direction of Ludhiana, with the intention of interfering with the advance of the British reinforcements.

On the 6th January, Sir John Grey arrived at the army head-quarters with a force of about 10,000 men, consisting of H.M.'s 9th and 16th Lancers, each over 500 strong; the 3rd Bengal Light Cavalry,

the 4th Irregular Cavalry, two Batteries of Artillery (12 guns), H.M.'s 10th Foot, and three regiments of Native Infantry with a company of Sappers. Leaving Meerut between the 10th and 16th December, they had marched over the fields of Moodkee and Ferozeshah still covered with the signs of the sanguinary battles which had there been fought also had been reinforced by the Sirmoor and Battalions of Goorkhas, the 30th Regiment Native, and one of cavalry under Brigadier Godby; whilst other troops were still on the march and closing up.

The Sikhs again assumed the initiative by crossing in a considerable body near Ludhiana for the purpose of gathering in supplies from their Jaghir states in that vicinity, and about Dhurmkote, a small fort halfway between Ferozeshah and Ludhiana, in which they had a garrison. On the 17th January, therefore, Sir Harry Smith was sent against this small fort, which was easily reduced, the garrison surrendering at discretion. But the Sikh force which had crossed the river, and which had been reinforced with all arms, now, under the Sirdar Runjoor Singh, threatened an attack on Ludhiana, and even indicated an intention of cutting our line of communication. Consequently, the Commander-in-chief decided to utilise Sir Harry Smith's force, strengthened by H.M.'s 16th Lancers, the 3rd Light Cavalry, a troop of Horse Artillery, and H.M.'s 53rd Foot (now on its way up and near Bussean), to relieve and secure Ludhiana.

Accordingly, on the 20th, Sir H. Smith marched from Dhurmkote of Jugraon, so as to skirt round Runjoor Singh, and so move by him into Ludhiana. On the 21st he advanced from Jugraon towards Ludhiana; but on approaching Budhowal, about 11 a.m., he found that Runjoor Singh had taken up an entrenched position which flanked and commanded the road by which he was moving. Being desirous of reaching Ludhiana without fighting a battle, he decided to move on across Runjoor's front, leaving him to be dealt with when the force was consolidated; and this brought on the affair of Budhowal, The Sikhs opened a heavy fire, but Smith moved on, covering his movement with his cavalry, artillery, and the 53rd Foot. The Sikh cavalry came out and followed up, cutting off a large portion of a baggage and a portion of the rearguard, but avoiding a conflict with our cavalry. Several European soldiers, exhausted by the long and arduous marches, were taken prisoners by the Sikhs, who, to their credit be it said, treated them fairly well, and, after the battle of Sobraon, released them and sent them back. Still, the number of killed and wounded, particularly in H.M.'s 53rd, proves that many stragglers, and probably sick men in the rear of the column, must have been mercilessly murdered. Quartermaster Cornes, who with a party of 1 sergeant, and 30 men of H.M.'s 53rd, was in charge of the regimental baggage, finding his party cut off from the main body, rallied round him a small detachment of the 16th Lancers and a party of sepoys, making in all 2 officers and 80 men; and succeeded in saving a considerable portion of the baggage, and making good his retreat on Jugraon, in the face of about 1000 Sikhs with a field-gun, who threatened to attack him, but were held in check by his bold front and steady discipline.

There are no official details of this affair; this account is taken principally from what can be gathered from regimental records. Sir Harry Smith, although he succeeded in passing by Runjoor Singh without fighting a general action, suffered a considerable loss in men and baggage, and marched into Ludhiana that evening, with his troops greatly exhausted. The 16th Lancers lost 2 men killed, and 1 wounded. H.M.'s 31st Regiment lost 21 men killed and wounded, and 19 taken prisoners. H.M.'s 53rd Regiment lost 36 men killed and 12 wounded. There is no means of ascertaining the loss of native troops. The Sikhs seem to have derived considerable encouragement from this skirmish; some highly exaggerated language about defeat and disaster was used by people who ought to have known better.

The Commander-in-chief also despatched the 2nd Brigade of Sir Harry Smith's Division on the 22nd January to reinforce him; the expulsion of the Sikhs from the Ludhiana neighbourhood being regarded as very important. Brigadier Wheeler, now recovered from the wound received at Moodkee, had resumed the command and reached Dhurmkote that evening, not having heard of the affair which had occurred at Budhowai on the previous day. On the 23rd he continued his march direct on Ludhiana, but on arriving at Sidham he gained information that a large Sikh force was on the road, and between him and the rest of the division. He therefore decided to return to Dhurmkote, and move round a circuitous way by Jugraon, his troops being fairly fagged out by their hard day's march. If over 30 miles through heavy sand arid under a hot sun. On the other hand, Runjoor Singh, hearing of Wheeler's advance, fed feeling that he might be attacked both from Dhurmkote and Ludhiana, made haste to evacuate his threatening position at Budhowal, and fell back on Aliwal close to the banks of the Sutlej. On the 24th Wheeler moved to Jugraon; on the 25th Sir Harry Smith advanced from Ludhiana to Budhowal, where; he was joined by Wheeler, and his whole force concentrated.

On the 26th, then, Sir Harry's whole force was made up as follows:-Artillery: 22 guns Horse Artillery, and 6 guns Field Artillery, under Major Lawrence. Cavalry - 1st Brigade, under Brigadier McDowell: H.M.'s 16th Lancers, 530 strong; 3rd Light Cavalry, 372; 4th Irregulars, 398 =

1300 men. 2nd Brigade,. under Brigadier Stedman: Governor-General's Body-guard, 351; 1st Light Cavalry, 422; 5th Light Cavalry, 402 = 1107 men. Cavalry of the Shekawatti Brigade, 631 men, under Major Forster; the whole cavalry force, under Brigadier Cureton of H.M.'s 16th Lancers, numbering 3038. Infantry – 1st Brigade, Brigadier Hicks commanding: H.M.'s 31st Regiment, now reduced to 544 men; 24th Regiment Native Infantry, 481 men; 36th Regiment Native Infantry, 571 men = 1596. 2nd Brigade (Brigadier Wheeler); H.M.'s 50th Regiment, 494 men only (sad results of Moodkee and Ferozeshah); 48th Native Infantry,. 857 men; and the Sirmoor Goorkhas, 781 men = 2132 3rd Brigade, under Brigadier Wilson: H.M.'s 53rd Regiment, 699; 30th Native Infantry, 824 Shekawatti Battalion, 625 4th Brigade, under Brigadier Godby: 47th Native Infantry, 713; the Nusseeree Battalion Goorkhas, 586 = 1299. Total infantry, 7175.

Sir Harry Smith's total force, therefore, amounted to more than 10,000 fighting men, with 28 field guns, and two 8-inch howitzers Sirdar Runjoor Singh, whose troops at Budhowal had been. chiefly irregular levies, had also received a reinforcement of 4000 regular troops and 12 guns, on the 26th.

Sir Harry Smith's men had gone through such long marches and such hard work that he considered it advisable to give them a day's rest to recruit themselves; but at daylight on the 28th January he advanced from Budhowal to attack Runjoor, who was known to be in position at Aliwal, on the left bank of the Sutlej, about 16 miles to the north-west, having a very considerable force and some 50 guns, and with every intention of fighting.

The cavalry in the line of columns, with two troops of Horse Artillery, formed the first line, and covered Sir Harry's front, scouting the country as they advanced, infantry and artillery following. After proceeding in this order about 9 miles, the enemy were sighted in position in the west of a low ridge about a mile in front. Sir Harry Smith had received information through spies that it was Runjoor Singh's intention to move out of his position that morning either on Ludhiana, or to attack him at Budhowal; and as he approached, this rumour was confirmed by a spy, who reported that the Sikh army was usually on the march. Sir Harry, however, felt confident that whatever movements Runjoor might be contemplating, he had him in his grasp now; and his continued advance direct upon the Sikhs brought them entirely to the defensive.

Runjoor took up a position with his left on the banks of the Sutlej, along the crest of some rising ground; the village of Aliwal was held somewhat in front of his left, and the village of Boondree on his right, his guns being placed all along the line of front, the general bearing of which was south-east. Sir Harry Smith's line faced north-west. As he approached Runjoor Singh the cavalry and horse artillery wheeled outwards, and took up position on the right and left, displaying the now deployed one of infantry advancing to the attack. The batteries immediately advanced to effective range, and came into action; and the battle began.

It was 10 o'clock, and the whole scene most striking. The morning was clear and beautiful, the country open end hard grass land - a fair field for all arms. There was no dust, and the sun shone brightly. Brigadier Stedman commanded the cavalry on the right; the 1st and with Regiments of Native Cavalry, the Governor-General's Bodyguard, the Shekawatti cavalry, and the 4th Irregulars. Then came Godby's Brigade, the Goorkhas of the Nusseeree Battalion, and the 36th Native Infantry; next, Hicks's Brigade, H.M.'s 31st Foot, with the 24th and 47th Regiments Native Infantry; on their left and in the centre of the line the two 8-inch howitzers and a large battery of 18 guns; then Wheeler's Brigade, H.M.'s 50th, the 48th Native Infantry, the Sirmoor Goorkhas (Brigadier Wheeler had so much confidence in his own regiment, the 48th that he placed it in the centre of the brigade : the corp fully justified his opinion); then two batteries of artillery (12 guns); then Wilson's Brigade of H.M.'s 53rd Foot the 30th Native Infantry, and the Shekawatti infantry then on the extreme left H.M.'s. 16th Lancers and the 3rd Light Cavalry.

Sir Harry Smith soon perceived that by bringing up his right, and carrying the village of Aliwal in front of the Sikh left, he could with great effect precipitate himself upon their left and centre, and cut off their line of retreat by the ford. He, therefore, brought up Godby's Brigade, and with it Hicks's. The latter was directed upon the village, which was carried in fine style, and two guns taken. At the same time the right brigade of cavalry was directed to attack the Sikh horse, and this also was most gallantly done, their cavalry being driven back upon and among their own infantry, while our right pushed on rapidly. Whilst these operations were going on on the right Brigadier Wheeler also advanced to the attack supported by Wilson; the guns of Alexander, Turton, Lane, Mill, Boileau, and of the Shekawatti Brigade, as also the 8-inch howitzers, pushing on continually in front of the advancing infantry. The enemy's fire fell heavily upon the right brigade – Wheeler's own - but they advanced most steadily, halting twice and lying down under the fire, to steady the men and prevent hurry, and to allow Wilson's Brigade to get forward; which was necessary because of the enemy's position being on a curve, with the flank thrown back. In this manner the advance continued until they were close upon the Sikhs. Meanwhile that brilliant cavalry commander, Brigadier Cureton, had been following up the infantry attack, watching keenly for his opportunity; and just as Wilson was preparing to charge the Sikh infantry and guns in front of him with H.M.'s 53rd and the Goorkhas and 30th Native Infantry, a thunder of horses' hoofs was heard on their left, and H.M.'s 16th Lancers, in great strength, came sweeping by with lances lowered, and, supported by the 3rd Bengal Light Cavalry, charged right down upon the foe. The Sikh infantry hurriedly formed squares; but the squadrons of the 16th swept through and through them, and smashing up a large body of the celebrated Aieen troops, trained by General Avitabile, utterly routed the whole Sikh right. The charge of one squadron of the 16th Lancers, led by Major Smyth and Captain Pearson, upon a well-formed square of Avitabile's Regiment, deserves special notice; as, notwithstanding the steadiness of the enemy, the Lancers broke the square, charged through, reformed and charged again in splendid style - a feat very rarely accomplished. Wheeler, with his own and Wilson's Brigades, followed up rapidly, with the result of capturing the village of Boondree and many guns; the village being stormed by H.M.'s 53rd. The Sikh infantry declined to meet the charge of Wilson's Brigade; but their gunners resolutely stood their ground. They could not, however, hold the guns, which were captured at the point of the bayonet. The whole Sikh force was now driven in utter rout and confusion to the ford. Pursued by the cavalry, who made repeated charges, and pressed by the infantry, they were unable to make any attempt to rally, and flinging themselves into the river, fled to the right bank, leaving all their guns, camp equipage, baggage, and stores to fall into the hands of the victors; 67 guns were amongst the captured trophies, and many camel-guns.

Sir Harry Smith bestowed well-deserved praise on the officers and men who had fought this brilliant action. Of the artillery he said, "Our guns and gunners, officers and men may be equalled, but cannot be excelled; no troops ever behaved more nobly, British and native, without distinction; the native cavalry vieing with H.M.'s 16th Lancers and striving to lead in the repeated charges. Throughout the day there was no hesitation, but a bold and intrepid advance; and thus it is our loss is comparatively small." On this occasion also the Field Hospital arrangements were efficiently and well carried out and the wounded well provided for.

Aliwal proved the utter inability of the Sikh army, even with double the number of men and guns, to make more than an honourable stand against British troops on a fair field. It showed also that the native troops, when not exhausted by hunger and fatigue, as they had been at Ferozeshah, could render invaluable support to the English regiments; and to this Sir Harry Smith in his despatches amply testified.

The loss in this well-fought battle was small, in all regiments except H M.'s 16th Lancers; they in their brilliant charges, against guns and well-trained infantry who fought to the death, suffered heavily. There were 2 officers and 57 men killed, 6 officers and 77 men wounded - making a total of 8 officers and 134 men; 66 horses were killed and 35 wounded. The 50th Foot also, which advanced against the Sikh central battery, suffered considerably; the native corps serving with them lost 5 officers wounded, 1 native officer and 15 men killed, 9 native officers and 75 men wounded.

The total loss of the force amounted to: killed 151, wounded 413 and missing 25 men=580.

The immediate result of the victory was the complete submission of the whole of the Sikh territory on the left bank; of the Sutlej, which was entirely evacuated by the enemy.

The news of the complete defeat of Runjoor Singh was received, as might be expected, with great joy by both Governor-General and Commander-in-chief. The former issued a general order announcing the victory, congratulating the commander and his force, and extolling their valour, discipline and skill in well-deserved terms. To the cavalry especially he gave great credit. To Brigadier Cureton, who commanded the cavalry, his thanks were more markedly given for the skill and intrepidity with which he had handled his force; since the admiration of the army had been elicited by the resolute charges of H.M.'s 16th Lancers, penetrating the Sikh squares with the gallant support of the 3rd Native Light Cavalry. The guns taken in addition to those already captured at Moodkee and Ferozeshah brought the total up to 143 pieces. At Aliwal, also; the two Goorkha regiments, not yet enrolled among the regular regiments of infantry, much distinguished themselves. By order of the Governor-General a royal salute was fired from the British camp, the bands raising the National Anthem. The Sikhs on the opposite bank, not to be outdone, followed suit with both; and their bands were heard playing "God save the Queen"!

Sobroan:
February 10th

Reinforcements of all arms had been moving up ever since the great battle of Ferozeshah, and now the whole army was concentrated for the decisive struggle on the banks of the Sutlej. The siege-train, with ammunition for the field-guns, reached the Commander-In-Chief's camp on the 7th of February; and on the 8th Sir Harry Smith, with his victorious division, marched into camp. Meantime the Sikhs had been as busy as bees strengthening their position, and were to be seen at work every day until it had assumed quite formidable proportions. Strong earthworks with deep ditches stretched in half-circle from bank to bank; behind these the river formed a loop; and across it, in order to maintain their communications, the Sikhs had thrown a bridge of boats. There was also a ford. In order still further to protect the bridge, interior lines of earthworks had been erected in succession; the position was. throughout armed with heavy guns, whilst batteries were placed on the north side of the river, more effectually to sweep the front, especially of their right, against an attack in that direction. The strongest part of the enemy's position was the centre, the weakest on their right, where the earthworks were less formidable.

The position had been most carefully reconnoitred, the proceedings of the Sikhs strictly watched, the plan of attack most deliberately thought out.

At one time a plan was considered of suddenly breaking

up from before Sobraon, and endeavouring to cross the Sutlej by surprise at the Ford of Gunda Singh Walla, and then advancing upon the Sikhs; but Sir Hugh Gough, after full consideration, decided against this, as in his opinion there was little chance of effecting a surprise, the Sikhs having full information of all our movements. Moreover, even if we did cross successfully, the Sikh army might easily fall back on Lahore, thereby increasing our difficulties, owing to the hostility of the people; and the war might possibly be thus converted into one of sieges. He fully recognised the strength of the Sikh position at Sobraon; but he judged that a defeat there would be fatal to them, and would be in all probability decisive of the war; and he resolved to make it so.

Accordingly he arranged at attack the enemy's extreme right, and, having penetrated there, to roll them up.

This plan was submitted to the Governor-General, who replied in the following cautious and guarded words, "If, upon the fullest consideration, the artillery can be brought into play, I recommend you to attack; if it cannot, and you anticipate a heavy loss, I would recommend you not to attempt it." Unhesitatingly Sir Hugh Gough accepted the responsibility. On the 9th of February orders were issued for the attack, and these were fully explained to the generals commanding.

In order the better to understand the delivery of the attack, it is advisable to enumerate the force now collected, reorganised, and disposed for attack.

Major-General Sir John Littler still held Ferozepore and watched the ferry over the Sutlej. Sir John Grey, with the 8th Light Cavalry, and the 41st, 45th, and 68th Regiments Native Infantry, held Attaree, watching fords west of Sobraon. Brigadier Wheeler also took no part in the battle of Sobraon, having been left, after Aliwal, in command of a detachment of native troops, to watch the fords of the Sutlej, and cover Ludhiana.

The main body was concentrated before Sobraon with the Commander-in-Chief.

Brigadier Smith commanded the engineers; and here it is fair to mention the fact, so honourable to Brigadier Irvine, a very distinguished engineer officer, who arrived in camp on the evening of the 9th, that the command would have devolved on him as senior officer; but that, with the generosity of spirit which is always a characteristic of a true-born soldier, he declined to assume it, in order that all the credit of the work which Brigadier Smith had begun might attach to that officer. For himself, Brigadier Irvine sought only to share the perils of the field, and throughout the day he accompanied the Commander-in-Chief.

Brigadier Gowan, C.B., commanded the artillery. An endeavour had been made to rectify the inferiority of our guns in the matter of weight of metal by enlarging the bores of nine-pounders into twelve; but the number of our guns did not exceed 60.

Major-General Sir Joseph Thackwell, a distinguished Peninsula and Waterloo officer, commanded the cavalry division; Brigadier Cureton commanded the greater part of the cavalry, H.M.'s 16th Lancers, with the 3rd, 4th, and 5th Regiments of Light Cavalry with which he was to make a show of crossing the Sutlej by the Hurreekee Ford, on the right flank of the attack, so as to draw the enemy's attention to that point.

Sir Harry Smith's Division of Infantry of two brigades, under Brigadier Penny and Brigadier Hicks respectively (the former consisting of H.M.'s 31st Foot, the 47th Native Infantry and the Nusseeree Battalion (Goorkhas); and the latter of H.M.'s 50th Foot and the 42nd Native Infantry), was to attack the enemy's extreme left; and formed on our right, supported by Campbell's Cavalry Brigade, which included H.M.'s 9th Lancers and two troops Horse Artillery.

The centre was occupied by Gilbert's Division of Infantry: 1st Brigade, under Brigadier Taylor, H.M.'s 29th Foot, the 41st and 68th Regiments Native Infantry; 2nd Brigade, the 1st European Light Infantry, the 16th Regiment Native Infantry and the Sirmoor Battalion (Goorkhas), under Brigadier McLaran. Between him and Sir Harry Smith on the right, was placed a battery of eight heavy guns. Gilbert's Division was accompanied by No. 19 Field Battery.

On Gilbert's left was to be placed another battery of heavy guns.

On the extreme left Sir Robert Dick was to lead the attack, and his force was strengthened accordingly; it was to advance in two lines, and to have a strong to have a strong reserve of both cavalry and infantry. **His first line consisted of H.M.'s 10th and 53rd Regiments, with the 43rd and 59th Regiments Native Infantry, Brigadier Stacey, accompanied by Brigadier Orchard. His second line was made up of H.M.'s 80th Foot, with the 33rd Native Infantry, under Brigadier Wilkinson; whilst in reserve were placed H.M.'s 9th Foot, the 62nd Foot, and the 26th Native Infantry, under Brigadier Hon. T. Ashburn-ham; and to their rear, again. Brigadier Scott's Cavalry Brigade, H.M.'s 3rd Light Dragoons, and the 3rd and 9th Irregulars, with whom were the 4th, 5th and 73rd Regiments Native Infantry.**

Fortune so far favoured the British that the river had suddenly risen owing to a storm of heavy rain which had occurred a day or two before; so much so that the ford, which was usually safe, had become extremely dangerous on the day of the attack.

At 2 a.m. the troops fell in silently, and, forming into columns, moved quietly towards their respective positions. No sound or sign of the coming attack reached the Sikhs, and, whilst it was yet dark, the various columns had all formed accurately according to their orders for the attack. There they waited, in disciplined order and silence, for the dawn of day. When it came, a dense fog so covered the ground that nothing could be seen, and it became necessary to wait yet longer; but presently the scene changed. In the animated language of the historical records of the 1st Bengal European Light Infantry, now the Royal Munster Fusiliers, evidently written by one who was present–

> *"The rising sun rapidly dispelled the fog, when a magnificent picture presented itself. The batteries of artillery were seen in position ready to open fire, and the plain covered with our troops, the fortified village of Rhoda Walla on our left rear being strongly held by our infantry. Immediately the guns opened a heavy fire. The enemy appearing suddenly to realise their danger, their drums beat the alarm, their bugles sounded to arms, and in a few minutes their batteries were manned and pouring shot and shell upon our troops."*

Thus quickly was the scene transformed from the picturesque to war in veritable earnest; and thus began the Battle of Sobraon.

For two hours the hail of shot and shell continued on both sides, and yet no decided advantage had been gained; the Sikh guns, firing from behind their field fortifications, could not be silenced. It was clear, as at Ferozeshah, that the battle could not be gained by superiority of artillery fire; the ammunition of the heavy guns was failing and their fire slackening. This was reported to the Commander-in-Chief, to whom it was evident that the issue of the struggle must be brought to "the arbitrament of musketry and the bayonet." He had the most implicit confidence in the ability and leading of his officers, and the courage and discipline of his troops. Turning to his nephew, Colonel

J. B. Gough, Quartermaster-General, he directed him to convey the order to Sir Robert Dick to commence the attack. In such moments as this the spirit of the commander communicates itself like magic to his troops, and a rumour flew down. the line at once "that old Gough had been told that there were only four more rounds left per gun, and says, 'Thank God ! then I'll be at them with the bayonet'." Whether he actually used those precise words or not is immaterial; the fact that the rumour went down the line is beyond any manner of doubt, and it was received with delight by the men, because they knew and felt there was not a doubt of success in their brave old leader's mind, and that he had most perfect confidence in them.

Sir Robert Dick received the order at nine o'clock, and immediately the batteries of Horsford, Fordyce, and Lane's Horse Artillery galloped to the front, and proceeded to cover the advance of Stacey's Brigade, which moved forward with the utmost steadiness, frequently halting to correct the line and prevent any hurry on the part of the men. The guns continued their advance in this manner, preceding the infantry, and taking up fresh positions till within 300 yards of the entrenchments, when a body of the enemy's cavalry moved out and threatened, the left flank of the line, where H.M.'s 53rd Foot was advancing. These were soon dispersed by a well-directed fire from the flank company of the regiment, and by the discharge of some rounds of grape from one of the batteries. The 53rd. immediately following up, with a cheer charged the enemy's entrenchments, being the first to enter them. During this advance the regiment was enfiladed for a time by a Sikh battery on the right bank of the river, Captain Warren being killed, and Lieutenant Lucas, carrying one of the colours, wounded. Stacey's Brigade rushed forward simultaneously, and the first line of the enemy's entrenchments was occupied.

Colonel Gough, who accompanied Sir Robert Dick's attack, here fell severely wounded. Stacey's attack was ably supported by Brigadier Wilkinson, not a shot having been fired, except by the flank campany, until the first line of entrenchments was carried.

Here, however, Stacey's advance was checked, and he had to wait until Dick brought up his second line, for the Sikh batteries to the right now enfiladed our troops. These were attacked and carried by H.M.'s 10th and 80th; Sir Robert Dick meeting his death-wound about this time. The division then continued its advance, driving the enemy towards the centre; the Sikh Akhalis (fanatics corresponding to the Mussulman Ghazis) fighting most stubbornly. Here a curious form of defence had been adopted by the enemy. Large pits capable of holding 30 men had been prepared, into which they were now crowded, and, being caught like rats in a trap, were easily disposed of.

The Sikhs, seeing that their right had been broken into, commenced a rush from all parts of their position to retake it. In order to hold them in check, and to relieve the pressure on Dick's Division, the divisions of Sir Harry Smith on the right, and Gilbert in the centre, were ordered to attack at once.

In the same manner as Dick had advanced, Sir Harry Smith led on his division against the extreme left of the Sikh position; Brigadier Penny in the first line, supported closely by Brigadier Hicks, and covered by the fire of the artillery. The men, who up to this had been lying down, sprang up, formed and advanced. But the ground immediately in front of the Sikh works was much broken by watercourses, which made it difficult for the men to keep their places; the enemy's fire was very severe, and the formidable nature of the earthworks prevented the assailants climbing up. After a desperate struggle, the first line was compelled to give way and fall back; but they were well and resolutely supported by Brigadier Hicks, who, opening the ranks to let the men through, re-formed and charged. Penny's Brigade, rapidly rallying, joined in the charge again, the soldiers being maddened by seeing the Sikhs run out and cut up their unfortunate and brave comrades who had fallen in the first attack. This time the entrenchments were carried. Brigadier Penny having been severely wounded in the first attack, Colonel Spence, of H.M.'s 31st, assumed command of the 1st Brigade.

Thus our troops had established themselves on the enemy's left flank, and were pressing on when a fire was opened on them from behind. Turning round, it was seen that some of the Sikhs had run in again on the captured guns and reopened fire; whereupon Hicks directed H.M.'s 50th to retake them, which was quickly done.

Gilbert's Division, in the centre, attacking at the same time as the first division under Smith, came upon such high earthworks that they were quite unable to scale them without ladders, and were twice forced to fall back. Not even their devoted gallantry could overcome the obstacles, and their loss was great. Gilbert himself was wounded, and Brigadier McLaran most severely. Major Fisher, of the Sirmoor battalion, was shot dead with a bullet in the brain; it is remarkable that he remained sitting on his horse for an appreciable interval before he fell. Many officers and men were struck down. Yet a third time the division was led on to the charge, on a part of the earthworks considerably to the left of the part previously attacked, where they were lower. Mounting on each other's shoulders, they gained a footing in the entrenchments, and as they increased in numbers they rushed upon the guns, which were now captured; and soon the glad news that all the troops had won their way into the Sikh position spread down the line. In this third charge fell also Brigadier Taylor, of H.M.'s 29th, struck by a bullet in the head, after he had already been wounded by a sabre-cut in the face.

H.M.'s 3rd Light Dragoons again greatly distinguished themselves by their exceptional gallantry. Following up Dick's Division, they found their way within the line of the entrenchments, and charged down among the now discomfited Sikhs; yet to the last the enemy fought bravely and doggedly, endeavouring to stem the torrent of retreat; but, pressed on all sides, they were forced headlong to the bridge. The guns now brought up opened a heavy and destructive fire; the bridge gave way under the fugitives, and no resource was left but the river, the deepened ford of which was no longer safe. Our troops, fairly infuriated by the butchery of their brave comrades massacred before their eyes, spared not, and it is calculated that the Sikh loss exceeded 10,000 men. Every gun within the position was captured, 67 guns, mostly of heavy calibre, being taken on the field, and the whole Sikh army was utterly and irretrievably defeated.

The action was completed before noon; but this great success was not achieved against a determined and resolute foe without a corresponding loss. Many brave and distinguished officers fell, foremost amongst them Sir Robert Dick, a veteran of the Peninsula and Waterloo; mortally wounded by a grape-shot in the moment of his glorious success, he died in the evening. Brigadier Taylor, of H.M.'s 29th, who had led his brigade so splendidly at Moodkee and Ferozeshah, was killed. Colonel Ryan, K.H., and Colonel Petit, both of H.M.'s 50th, were severely wounded. Colonel J.B. Gough and Colonel Barr, on the Commander-in-Chief's staff, Brigadier Penny, and Brigadier McLaran, were all severely wounded. Altogether, the killed numbered 320, and the wounded 2063.

Sir Henry Hardinge did not take any actual command on this occasion, but his fine military spirit led him into the thick of the battle, and he followed up the attack in person, encouraging the troops by his noble example.

Survey of the Campaign

Sobroan virtually terminated the war. The disaster to the Khalsa was complete and overwhelming. The Governor-General was now able to march, without meeting further resistance, upon Lahore, and there to dictate his own terms. In the next chapter we shall turn again to the political side of affairs, during the campaign and after it. Before doing so, however, we shall here pass in review certain aspects of the campaign itself.

On and about December 11th, 1845, the Sikh army crossed the Sutlej. The soldiery were the most stubborn we ever fought in India. Their guns were heavier and more numerous than ours, and were admirably served. At every stage our troops were greatly outnumbered; yet, within two months, four pitched battles were fought, and the enemy's army shattered; and another week saw the submission of Lahore to the Governor-General.

It is difficult to do even bare justice to the conduct of the troops engaged. The Umballa men were moving within 24 hours of receiving their marching orders. Over a rough country, heavy, sandy, amid clouds of dust, under a blazing sun, with little water, and often very inadequate food - for camels move slowly, and bullock-carts more slowly still, so that the cooking-utensils often arrived too late to allow of proper cooking - they marched 150 miles in seven days. They had already covered twenty miles on the day when they first came in collision with the enemy, whom they then put to rout after a stubborn resistance, capturing 17 guns. Three days later, having commenced their march at two o'clock in the morning, and having been for 14 hours already under arms, and almost without food, they stormed the Sikh entrenchments at Ferozeshah, and, despite a desperate resistance, would assuredly have carried them completely had not the fall of darkness made it necessary to draw off. The strain of the night which followed, with the bitter cold, the continued want of food and water, the incessant firing and yelling of the Sikhs, the uncertainty as to the fate of their comrades, was tremendous. Yet, when morning came, worn, and exhausted as they were, they renewed the attack with undaunted courage, swept the enemy's entrenchments clear at the point of the bayonet, put them to flight, and faced without flinching the fresh army which Tej Singh led from Ferozepore.

The courage, endurance, and discipline displayed were beyond all praise. The victories of Aliwal and Sobraon were brilliant, but they were fought under far more favourable conditions. In every case, indeed, we had foemen worthy of our steel; disciplined troops, fighting behind entrenchments with dogged resolution, well armed, well supplied with artillery, and superior in numbers to our own. But at Aliwal and Sobraon we fought with a moral assurance of winning. The task was hard, but the event was never really in doubt. Whereas at Ferozeshah, from the moment when it became evident that the falling darkness must prevent the completion of the victory so nearly won, the event was very doubtful indeed. These are the conditions which put the highest military qualities to the sternest test, and our men passed the ordeal with magnificent spirit.

Ferozeshah showed emphatically the superior quality of the European troops as compared with the sepoys. There the latter, with less stamina, seemed to have lost nerve as they became exhausted, did nothing like their share of the fighting, and might have broken down but for the stubbornness of their British comrades. At Sobraon and Aliwal, where they came to their work fresh and confident, no such reproach could be laid to their charge and they won their full measure of enthusiastic praise.

Of the British regiments which took part in this campaign, it may, indeed, be said that every one covered itself with glory. No cavalry regiment have ever surpassed the feats achieved by H.M.'s 3rd Light Dragoons. At Moodkee they entered into action 494 strong; their killed and wounded there numbered 101. Out of their diminished numbers, in their grand charge at Ferozeshah, when they swept right through the Sikh batteries and camp, they lost 148 men; altogether, just half their original strength, in the two engagements. Nor did they fail to distinguish themselves once more at Sobraon, where there fell 31 of their reduced band, and Sir Hugh Gough referred to them as a regiment "whom no obstacle usually held formidable by horse appears to check." At Moodkee, indeed, it seems likely that if they had been supported by a second and third line of such cavalry as the 9th and 16th Lancers, there would have been little left for any one else to do.

The 16th Lancers (part of the reinforcements from Meerut) won their laurels at Aliwal, where the notable achievement of the squadron which broke a Sikh square, charging clean through it, has been duly recorded. It certainly seems peculiarly unfortunate that, owing to the political exigencies before referred to, the Governor-General had found himself unable to order them to the front in time to take their part in the earlier engagements. Their losses at Aliwal were heavy : 2 officers and 57 men killed, 8 officers and 134 men wounded. At Sobraon, however, they were posted on the right, where the cavalry were not called upon to take any active part in the battle, and their losses were nil.

The 9th Foot, at Ferozeshah, after Reid's Brigade had already been repulsed, stormed and captured the same batteries, losing 265 killed and wounded out of a little over 800 of all ranks. Two distinguished old officers of the regiment, Sir John M'Caskill and Colonel Taylor, were killed at its head in the course of the war.

The 29th Foot, in spite of great exertions and hard marching, did not reach the Umballa force till after Moodkee; but at Ferozeshah, the former led the attack on the right, losing 250 of all ranks out of 758 engaged; and at Sobraon, after three desperate assaults, they again, in company with the 1st Europeans, stormed the Sikh entrenchments, losing 171 men out of the 513 which completed their muster on that morning; Colonel Taylor in command, than whom there was no better officer killed that day, fell in the third charge. When the brief campaign was over, they could scarcely turn out 350 men.

The 1st European Light Infantry, like the 29th, joined the army too late for Moodkee, after marching about 190 miles in, 8 days, but were in the thick of the fight at Ferozeshah, losing 51 men killed and 164 wounded, 215 in all, out of a strength of about 650 in the field. At Sobraon they mustered not much more than 400 in the field, of whom they lost 197 killed and wounded. Brigadier McLaran, who commanded the brigade on both occasions, fell mortally wounded at their head, at Sobraon; an officer greatly beloved and respected by all who served under him. In recognition of its conspicuous gallantry and distinguished services, the regiment was granted, on the recommendation of the Commander-in-Chief, the honourable title of "1st Bengal Fusiliers," which, again, has given place to their present name, "The Royal Munster Fusiliers." So severe had been the duty, so nobly did they perform it, that, on the 11th of February, the day after Sobraon, this regiment was only able to muster 6 officers and 230 men fit for duty, a casualty roll rarely parlleled by any regiment in a successful campaign.

H.M.'s 31st and 50th Regiments served in Sir Harry Smith's Division, and were present at Moodkee, Ferozeshah, Aliwal and Sobraon. At the first of these battles, where the brunt of the fighting fell on Smith's Division, the 31st lost 9 officers and 155 men killed or wounded out of 30 officers and 844 men taken into action. At Ferozeshah, in the two days, there fell 8 officers and 151 men more. At Budhowal 21 men more were killed or wounded, and 19 men taken prisoners by the Sikhs; these, however, were released after Sobraon. At Aliwal it lost 16 men, and at Sobraon 6 officers and 137 men, making a loss in the campaign of 503 out of a total strength of not more than 900. The 50th, a regiment of Peninsular fame, maintained its noble record. At Moodkee there fell 6 officers and 129 men; at Ferozeshah 6 officers, 113 rank and file, out of a strength of about 700 men. Although before Aliwal they were joined by a draft of 5 young officers and 90 men, they could not muster more than 494 men for that battle, where they lost 10 officers and 68 men killed and wounded; while at Sobraon there fell 197 of all ranks, including 12 officers. Colonel Ryan, who commanded the regiment with great ability throughout the campaign, fell dangerously wounded at Sobraon, dying of his wound not long after. Every one of the senior officers was disabled early in the fight, the command of the regiment devolving upon a subaltern, Lieutenant Wiley, and nearly half the men fell. To add to the mournful roll, a terrible calamity overtook this same regiment shortly after its return from the campaign, the barracks occupied by them at Ludhiana being blown down in a violent storm on the night of May 20, 1846, when 80 men, women and children were killed and 135 seriously wounded. During the campaign almost every officer was wounded, the total loss amounting to 565 killed and wounded of all ranks.

The 80th Regiment were engaged at Moodkee, Ferozeshah and Sobraon. At the first action they lost 5 men killed, 1 officer and 19 men wounded; at Ferozeshah, 4 officers 32 men killed, 4 officers 73 men wounded, besides 7 privates returned "missing", who were never seen again, and were undoubtedly killed; in all 127 casualties. A detachment, 1 officer and 23 men, on the march up to join the army, took part in the Battle of Aliwal, losing 6 men killed and 1 wounded. At Sobraon they lost 13 men killed, 4 officers 74 men wounded; during the whole campaign, 250 casualties of all ranks.

The 62nd lost heavily at Ferozeshah, 18 officers and 281 men falling in their assault upon the Sikh batteries; and at Sobraon they lost 1 officer killed, 1 officer 45 men wounded; total loss, 346 Records do not show what strength the regiment took into action, but it is probable that the number at Ferozeshah did not exceed 800 men.

The 53rd Foot did not appear on the field of battle until after Ferozeshah. They were attached to Sir Harry Smith's force and took part in the relief of Ludhiana. At Budhowal they formed the rear-guard, and covered the movement on Ludhiana, losing 36 men killed and 12 wounded. At Aliwal the regiment appears to have gone into action 699 strong; their small loss, 6 men killed and 8 wounded, being due to the admirable manner in which the regiment advanced upon the Sikh batteries, running forward at the double for about 100 yards, then lying down and advancing again, by which manoeuvre the Sikh gunners were prevented from getting the range, and the men advanced both rapidly and steadily, without getting exhausted. At Sobraon, the loss was 1 officer and 6 men killed, 8 officers 112 men wounded; total, 189, out of a strength of about 700.

H.M.'s 10th Foot took part in the crowning victory of Sobraon, where the extreme steadiness of its advance, under that strict disciplinarian, Colonel Franks, attracted universal notice and admiration. Their loss amounted to 10 officers 27 men killed, 2 officers 101 men wounded.

Of the native troops engaged, few remain now on the rolls of the Indian army, almost all having been swept away in the vortex of the great Mutiny of 1857; but their services in this campaign cannot be disregarded or unrecognised. It is true that neither at Moodkee nor at Ferozeshah were they equal to the occasion, but this was undoubtedly owing to the frightful exhaustion of the sepoys, who had not the same stamina and physical endurance as the British soldier. Both at Aliwal and Sobraon they fought well, and bore their fair share of the loss, affording valuable support of their European comrades. Records do not give the various losses by regiments, but simply abstracts of the loss sustained by divisions, including Europeans and natives, in one total. What the native regiments suffered can only be approximately calculated by deducting the losses of the European regiments as taken from their records.

Sir Harry Smith spoke in warm terms of the conduct of the native troops, both cavalry and infantry, at Aliwal, and both Governor-General and Commander-in-Chief were able to applaud their conduct at Sobraon. The Goorkhas, a regiment of which, the Sirmoor battalion, is now represented by the 2nd Prince of Wales's Own Goorkhas, distinguished themselves particularly in the two last engagements, and were specially mentioned by Sir Hugh Gough at Sobraon. They were not present at Moodkee or Ferozeshah. Of the other native infantry regiments the only survivors now existing in the Indian army are the 4th Bengal Infantry (formerly 33rd), the 5th (formerly

42nd), the 6th (formerly 43rd), the 7th (formerly 47th), the 8th (formerly 59th) and the 9th (formerly 63rd) Native Infantry.

The campaign of the Sutlej throws us back in touch with the soldiers of the Peninsula and Waterloo, many of whom were here in high command. Besides Sir Henry Hardinge and Sir Hugh Gough, both of whom gained high distinction under Wellington, Sir Harry Smith, Sir Robert Sale, Sir John McCaskill, Sir Robert Dick, Sir Joseph Thackwell, Brigadier Cureton, and Brigadier Taylor, of H.M.'s 29th, all served in the Peninsula. Of these, McCaskill, Sale, Dick and Taylor fell gloriously for Queen and country, after long lives spent in honourable service. Amongst the most distinguished officers whose loss was to be deplored was Major Broadfoot, chief political officer to the Governor-General. General Gilbert, whose services were highly appreciated by the Commander-in-chief,. and who led his division with such intrepidity and ability, was a grand old soldier of the Indian army. He was passionately found of riding and horses, and a distinguished performer on the pig-skin, both on the turf and in the pigsticking field. So devoted was he to this sport that during the period when the army was lying encamped in front of Sobraon, he, with a few congenial spirits, used to hunt the jungles for wild boar, riding close up to the Sikh outposts in pursuit of his game, while they never offered to molest or interfere with him. He subsequently served with equal distinction and credit, as will hereafter be related, in the second Sikh War, and it was to him that eventually the Sikh army, in 1849, surrendered and laid down their arms.

In considering the course of the whole campaign, certain points deserve special attention. Emphasis has already been laid strongly on the nature of the odds against which it was conducted. The quality of the Sikh troops was such that they showed themselves behind entrenchments hardly, if at all, inferior to average European soldiery. Insubordinate as they had been politically, their discipline and steadiness on the field were admirable. Their muskets were the same as ours, their artillery usually superior and their fire directed with precision. Such a foe could not be beaten without heavy losses on our part. It would even seem that if they had shown the same capacity for attack as for defence, if Tej Singh had known what to do with his fresh army at Ferozeshah, the frontier force with the Governor-General and the Commander-in-Chief might have been crushed on December 22nd. It is evident that if the nature of the struggle before us had been realised, if it had not been. credited that there was a real chance of averting the war altogether, and that the Sikh troops were too insubordinate to be dangerous, so small a force ought never to have been left to bear unsupported the brunt of such a contest,

But the hope that war might be avoided, coupled with the consciousness that preparations on at all a large scale, and especially any palpable increase of the frontier force, would certainly precipitate a conflict, counted for more than the urgent representations of the military authorities. When the great Sikh host crossed the Sutlej, it became absolutely necessary to make an instant advance, with all available troops, to save Ferozepore and Bussean. To wait for troops from Meerut would have meant the loss of those important places. Consequently, when the available troops got to Ferozeshah,. there were not enough of them, in the Governor-General's opinion, to attack the entrenchments until Littler should arrive.

Rightly or wrongly, the attack was in consequence deferred till late in the day; and further comment on the highly critical position which resulted would be superfluous, after what has been said.

Under such conditions, to have literally crumpled up the army of the Khalsa within two months of the declaration of war was no small achievement. But if the conduct of the British troops, from highest to lowest, deserves all praise, no little praise also is due to our valiant and stubborn foe. The admiration they inspired in the heart of one who knew how to appreciate their qualities may well be expressed in Sir Hugh Gough's own words, referring to the slaughter of the Sikh army at Sobraon. "Policy," he wrote, "prevented my publicly recording my sentiments of the splendid gallantry of a fallen foe, and I declare, were it not from a conviction that my country's good required the sacrifice, I could have wept to have witnessed the fearful slaughter of so devoted a body." It was indeed fortunate for us that the leaders were not worthy of the men, that Taj Singh was faint-hearted, and Lall Singh incompetent and only half trusted; that, while the chiefs were not unskilful in disposing their troops behind entrenchments, none of them bad the training or the skill in manoeuvring large bodies of men which would have enabled them to reap the full benefit of a temporary advantage. That is no doubt the reason why the Sikhs, in face of the British troops, invariably adopted the defensive attitude, retiring under Tej Singh before Ferozeshah, and failing to make a real attack even at Budhowal, where the consequences might well have been very serious.

But when all is said, the whole campaign shows very conclusively one fact, which always appears to be a source of astonishment to the British public - that if we have to do battle with an enemy whose army is highly disciplined, well armed, and game to fight till it can fight no longer, that army cannot be beaten without correspondingly heavy losses, and demands treatment considerably more respectful than Clive found it necessary to show for the mercenary troops of Surajah Dowlah or Chunda Sahib. Also, that it is a mistake to take for granted that "Native" opponents must be lacking in those high qualities.

ALSO FROM LEONAUR
AVAILABLE IN SOFTCOVER OR HARDCOVER WITH DUST JACKET

EW2 EYEWITNESS TO WAR SERIES
CAPTAIN OF THE 95th (Rifles) *by Jonathan Leach*
An officer of Wellington's Sharpshooters during the Peninsular, South of France and Waterloo Campaigns of the Napoleonic Wars.

SOFTCOVER : **ISBN 1-84677-001-7**
HARDCOVER : **ISBN 1-84677-016-5**

WF1 THE WARFARE FICTION SERIES
NAPOLEONIC WAR STORIES
by Sir Arthur Quiller-Couch
Tales of soldiers, spies, battles & Sieges from the Peninsular & Waterloo campaigns

SOFTCOVER : **ISBN 1-84677-003-3**
HARDCOVER : **ISBN 1-84677-014-9**

EW1 EYEWITNESS TO WAR SERIES
RIFLEMAN COSTELLO *by Edward Costello*
The adventures of a soldier of the 95th (Rifles) in the Peninsular & Waterloo Campaigns of the Napoleonic wars.

SOFTCOVER : **ISBN 1-84677-000-9**
HARDCOVER : **ISBN 1-84677-018-1**

MC1 THE MILITARY COMMANDERS SERIES
JOURNALS OF ROBERT ROGERS OF THE RANGERS *by Robert Rogers*
The exploits of Rogers & the Rangers in his own words during 1755-1761 in the French & Indian War.

SOFTCOVER : **ISBN 1-84677-002-5**
HARDCOVER : **ISBN 1-84677-010-6**

AVAILABLE ONLINE AT
www.leonaur.com
AND OTHER GOOD BOOK STORES

ALSO FROM LEONAUR
AVAILABLE IN SOFTCOVER OR HARDCOVER WITH DUST JACKET

RGW1 RECOLLECTIONS OF THE GREAT WAR 1914 - 18
STEEL CHARIOTS IN THE DESERT by S. C. Rolls

The first world war experiences of a Rolls Royce armoured car driver with the Duke of Westminster in Libya and in Arabia with T.E. Lawrence.

SOFTCOVER : **ISBN 1-84677-005-X**
HARDCOVER : **ISBN 1-84677-019-X**

RGW2 RECOLLECTIONS OF THE GREAT WAR 1914 - 18
WITH THE IMPERIAL CAMEL CORPS IN THE GREAT WAR by Geoffrey Inchbald

The story of a serving officer with the British 2nd battalion against the Senussi and during the Palestine campaign.

SOFTCOVER : **ISBN 1-84677-007-6**
HARDCOVER : **ISBN 1-84677-012-2**

EW3 EYEWITNESS TO WAR SERIES
THE KHAKEE RESSALAH
by Robert Henry Wallace Dunlop

Service & adventure with the Meerut Volunteer Horse During the Indian Mutiny 1857-1858.

SOFTCOVER : **ISBN 1-84677-009-2**
HARDCOVER : **ISBN 1-84677-017-3**

WF1 THE WARFARE FICTION SERIES
NAPOLEONIC WAR STORIES
by Sir Arthur Quiller-Couch

Tales of soldiers, spies, battles & Sieges from the Peninsular & Waterloo campaigns

SOFTCOVER : **ISBN 1-84677-003-3**
HARDCOVER : **ISBN 1-84677-014-9**

AVAILABLE ONLINE AT
www.leonaur.com
AND OTHER GOOD BOOK STORES

www.ingramcontent.com/pod-product-compliance
Lightning Source LLC
Chambersburg PA
CBHW021004090426
42738CB00007B/649